Bandana-rama

WRAP GLUE SEW

21 Fast & Fun Craft Projects
Headbands, Skirts, Pillows & More

JUDITH CRESSY

FunStitch
STUDIO
stitch your art out.

Text copyright © 2014 by Judith Cressy

Photography and Artwork copyright © 2014 by C&T Publishing, Inc.

PUBLISHER: Amy Marson

CREATIVE DIRECTOR: Gailen Runge

ART DIRECTOR: Kristy Zacharias

EDITOR: Lee Jonsson

TECHNICAL EDITORS: Ann Haley and Gailen Runge

COVER/BOOK DESIGNER: April Mostek

PRODUCTION COORDINATOR: Rue Flaherty

PRODUCTION EDITOR: Katie Van Amburg

ILLUSTRATOR: Jessica Jenkins

PHOTO ASSISTANT: Mary Peyton Peppo

STYLED PHOTOGRAPHY by Nissa Brehmer, unless otherwise noted
INSTRUCTIONAL PHOTOGRAPHY by Diane Pedersen, unless otherwise noted

Published by FunStitch Studio, an imprint of C&T Publishing, Inc., P.O. Box 1456, Lafayette, CA 94549

Concept by Robie Rogge

Library of Congress Cataloging-in-Publication Data

Cressy, Judith.

 Bandana-rama : wrap, glue, sew : 21 fast & fun craft projects : headbands, skirts, pillows & more / Judith Cressy.

   pages cm

Includes index.

ISBN 978-1-60705-921-9 (soft cover)

1. Bandannas. 2. Dress accessories--Patterns. 3. Sewing. 4. Handicraft. I. Title.

TT667.5.C74 2014

745.5--dc23

                    2014008133

Printed in China

10 9 8 7 6 5 4 3 2 1

CONTENTS

DEDICATION

To Wooflet, for believing

And to Robie, for opening doors

Introduction

How many fashion accessories have been shared by outlaws and preppies, pirates, cowgirls, hippies, and ninja turtles? Only one that I can think of—the bandana. It's been a wardrobe classic for more than 200 years and shows no signs of disappearing.

On these pages you'll find ideas for turning bandanas into tops, skirts, belts, bags, and headbands, as well as a few things for decorating your room. Some of the projects require nothing more than scissors and glue, but if you're ready to sew, you'll discover that bandanas are a great place to start. They're already hemmed, so projects go together quickly, and the printed borders make cutting and following stitching lines easy. This book includes projects for all skill levels; some can be made with a single bandana. By combining colors and mixing and matching border patterns, you'll be creating one-of-a-kind designs of your own in no time.

Also on these pages, you'll learn a few hand-sewing basics, which are at the heart of all dressmaking and craft needlework. Even when you do most of your sewing on the machine, from time to time you'll still need to pick up a needle and thread to repair a hem, baste a seam, or sew on a button. In other words, you'll find many uses for these simple stitches.

Enjoy!
Judith

Who doesn't love bandanas!

Bandana Basics

A *little history* ... *and everything else you need to know.*

A LITTLE HISTORY

When the first Indian silk scarves showed up in European shops in the 1600s, everyone had to have one. The brilliantly colored scarves were woven with a fluid teardrop design called the *boteh*. No one in Europe had seen anything like it—it was so exotic—and merchants could barely keep up with the demand. The scarves were known as "bandanas," from the Sanskrit word *bandhana*, which means "to tie."

By the 1700s, French and British manufacturers were printing their own versions of the designs onto cotton scarves, which were as popular as the originals. In fact, one cotton-weaving center in Scotland, the town of Paisley, became so identified with the scarves that the *boteh* teardrop shape took on the name of the town.

After the American cotton industry was launched around 1800, manufacturers in the United States began producing their own bandanas. They've been with us ever since—equally at home on the range, on the railroads, at casual summer picnics, and on fashion photo shoots—no longer exotic, but beloved and wildly popular just the same.

EVERYTHING ELSE YOU NEED TO KNOW

Size and Shape

Some bandanas are the size of a handkerchief; others are large enough to wear as a sarong. The standard size is a 22″ square. All of the projects in this book are made with standard bandanas. With that said, you'll soon discover that bandanas are never truly square and they never measure exactly 22″ (in fact, each of the four sides of a bandana might be a slightly different measurement). The border designs (along each side) can also vary in width on a single bandana. This can be frustrating when you're trying to line up border patterns, but try to work around it. Part of the bandana's charm, after all, is its casual look.

Washing and Ironing

Most bandanas are 100% cotton, which is one of the nicest fabrics to work with. If you're not certain whether your bandana will shrink or if the colors will run in the wash, you'll want to check before you start your project. (If you're making a headband or something else that will never be washed, you can skip this step.)

Wash the bandana in hot water by itself or with other like colors. Tumble it dry in a hot dryer. It will definitely need ironing afterward. If you need help, be sure to ask an adult! Press the bandana with a steam iron on the cotton setting. If you want the bandana to be as crisp as it was before washing, spritz it with spray starch several times as you iron it.

Fraying

The most common fabric for bandanas is loosely woven cotton muslin, which frays (unravels) easily after it has been cut. Cutting bandanas with pinking shears will help prevent fraying. For a more permanent solution, use fusible (iron-on) interfacing on the back of the bandana, and finish edges with hems or blanket stitching.

Reversibility

Typically, bandanas are printed on both sides. They appear to be reversible, but one side often has better-quality printing than the other (usually the side without the hem fold). Throughout this book, I call these the *right side* and the *wrong side* of the bandana. For some projects, it's important to have the right side showing, so be sure to take a look before you sew.

Tools and Materials

The tools and materials used in this book can be found at most sewing and craft stores and through online suppliers. See Supplies and Resources (page 126) for additional information.

Chalk pencil: Use a chalk pencil to draw cutting or sewing lines on fabric. You can sharpen a chalk pencil in a regular pencil sharpener to draw a fine line. Later, you can erase the line with a damp cloth. An erasable fabric marker works well, too.

Darning needle: Few people do much darning (mending holes in fabric) any more, but oversize darning needles have large eyes, so they are just the tools you'll need if you are sewing a blanket stitch or other detail with yarn.

Dressmaker's pins: Always keep a pincushion full of pins close at hand. You'll need them constantly. I like glass- or pearl-head pins best because they're the easiest to grab.

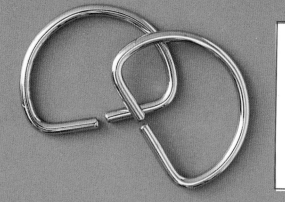

D-rings: Just as their name suggests, these belt rings, found in button and fabric shops, are D-shaped. Two rings are needed for making an adjustable belt. In a pinch, circular binder rings, found in any stationery store, will work just as well for a belt buckle.

Embroidery floss: Used for decorative handwork and edging, embroidery floss comes in a gorgeous array of glossy colors. It's sold in skeins of six threads that are loosely twisted together. To use it, cut the length you want, and then separate and pull out the number of strands you need.

Fabric marker: Use these disappearing-ink pens to mark stitching or cutting lines on fabric. Moisten the marks with a damp cloth and the ink will disappear. Be sure to store markers with the cap on tight and the tip pointed downward to prevent drying. A chalk pencil (page 8) also works well for marking.

Glue gun: An electric glue gun uses heat to melt sticks of glue. Its trigger allows you to squeeze out one dab of hot glue at a time. The melted glue hardens the moment it reaches its target, so you get an instant bond. Choose a low-temperature glue gun to avoid burns. Carefully follow the directions that come with it.

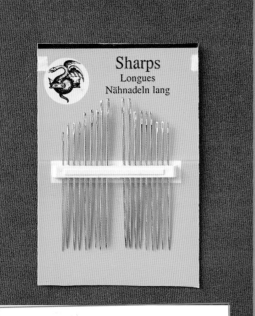

Interfacing: Interfacing is ironed or stitched to the back of your fabric to make it firmer. It gives body and support to the main fabric, such as inside a collar or cuffs. In this book, the projects that include interfacing use a lightweight, woven, fusible type. Fusible interfacings are ironed onto the wrong side of the fabric. After they are ironed into place, they can be treated as part of the fabric.

Hand needles: There are many types of needles for hand sewing. A package of general-purpose "sharps" in multiple sizes is fine for all the projects in this book. Use the size that feels most comfortable to you.

Leather punch: This hand-squeezed tool has a wheel with punches of different sizes. Turn the wheel to pick the size for the hole you need.

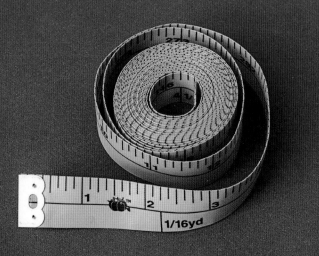

No-roll elastic: This heavyweight woven elastic comes in many widths. It will stay flat through its lifetime of washings and wearings, making it perfect for waistbands. Look for no-roll elastic in fabric stores with good notions departments.

Measuring tape: A flexible measuring tape is essential for taking body measurements. Use a yardstick or ruler when you have to measure and draw straight lines.

Pinking shears: The sawtooth blades of this type of scissor leave a zigzag cut. The zigzag will help to prevent fabric from fraying and make an attractive finished edge.

Seam ripper: This finely pointed tool is designed for cutting and picking out stitches without damaging the fabric. Be careful—it's sharp! You'll also find it handy for removing a scratchy label from store-bought clothing.

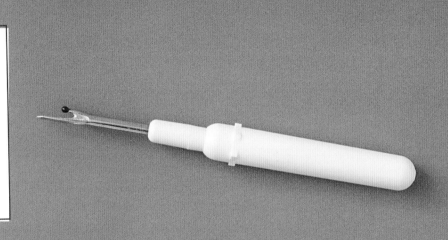

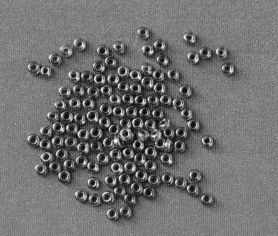

Seed beads: These tiny glass beads are just the thing for attaching sequins to fabric. They're available in an enormous range of iridescent and solid colors and are sold in small plastic tubes or bags in craft and sewing stores.

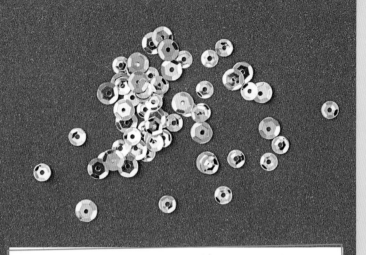

Sequins: Also called paillettes, these nearly weightless sparklers are available in a variety of sizes and shapes and a huge range of colors. If you're not sure which to choose, many craft and sewing stores carry them in mixed bags. Although sequins appear to be metal, they are actually plastic. Wash sequined articles in cold water, and keep them away from hot dryers and irons.

Thimble: A thimble is designed to fit over a fingertip to prevent it from being pricked while you sew by hand. A thimble is also handy when you need to push a needle through a dense thickness of fabric. Thimbles come in many sizes, so be sure to choose one that fits your finger snugly.

Turning tool: The tip of this tool comes to a gentle point. It is inserted inside a sewn article to push out the seams in tight corners or to push stuffing into a small opening.

Alex Anderson

Machine Basics

Although most home sewing machines perform the same general functions, they're all set up a little differently.

I've labeled some of the main parts here to explain their use, but be sure to read the manual that came with your machine for specifics on how to thread it, operate it, and maintain it.

A **Forward–reverse control:** Hold this lever (or button) down to go backward. Leave it in the up position to go forward. This control is particularly useful when you lock in the stitches at the beginning and end of a seam.

B **Handwheel:** Turning this wheel forward by hand allows you to raise and lower the needle as slowly as you like. You will use the handwheel when you make a right angle in a seam or when you need to ease in the needle very close to a point.

C **Bobbin-winder stopper:** The bobbin—the spool for the bottom thread—is wound on top of the machine. The bobbin-winder stopper is a little mushroom-shaped button that signals for the winding to stop when the bobbin is full.

D **Spool pins:** Spools of thread are set over these pins for sewing and bobbin winding.

E **Stitch selector:** This dial or panel of buttons allows you to select what gauge (length) stitch you want to use as well as the style of stitch. All of the projects in this book use a straight stitch, most at medium gauge. The two projects that require gathering use a wide gauge (the longest stitch).

F **Tension control:** This dial regulates the tension of the top thread. The tension, or tightness, of the top and bottom threads needs to be kept in balance for perfect stitches.

G **Thread guide for bobbin winding:** As the name suggests, you will wrap the thread from the spool around this tiny wheel when you wind a bobbin.

H **Take-up lever:** This lever helps to control the flow and tension of the thread as you sew.

I **Thread guides:** These wire clips keep the thread lined up toward the machine's needle as you sew.

J **Presser foot screw:** This large screw allows you to change the machine's foot. There are several different kinds of feet, two of which are used for projects in this book.

K **Presser foot:** The presser foot is used for almost all regular sewing needs. Its broad width helps feed the fabric through the machine evenly. It is designed to rock lightly, allowing it to adjust to varied thicknesses, such as gathered fabric. The machine's zipper foot, in contrast, is narrower and is adjustable side to side. Use the zipper foot when you need to stitch very close to an edging—or a zipper, of course. Raise and lower the foot by means of a lever, usually found right behind it.

L **Bobbin case:** The bobbin is inserted below the needle and presser foot. The thread from the bobbin feeds upward for the bottom stitches.

M **Foot pedal:** The foot pedal is the control center of the machine. Nothing happens until you press your foot on this pedal. Use a light touch! Not only does the pedal operate the machine, but it also controls the speed. You might stitch faster in the middle of a seam but slower at either end. Before you start your project, give the pedal a test drive on some scraps of fabric to get a feel for the pressure you will want to apply.

After your first few tries sewing on a machine, you will start to feel at home with it. Treat the machine gently and it will treat you well in return.

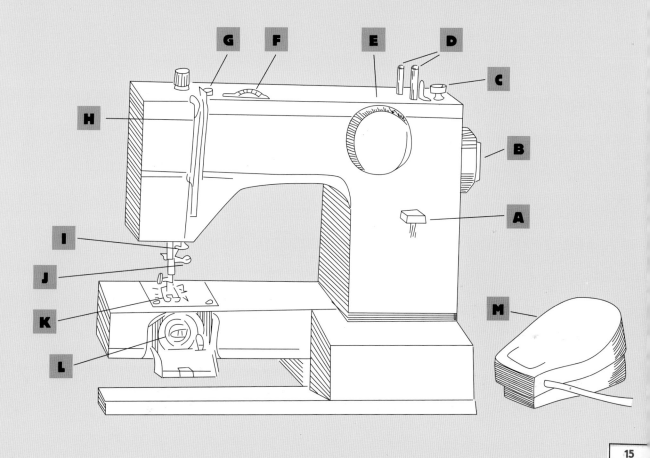

OTHER BITS TO KNOW

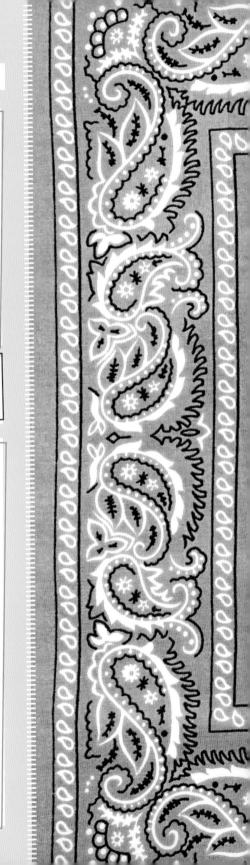

Sewing machine needles: Machine needles come in many sizes, with different styles of points for different types of fabrics. For work on bandanas and most other woven fabrics, choose a normal, or *universal,* sharp-point needle, size 11–14. The needle packaging will list the appropriate fabrics. Keep an extra package on hand. Needles can break or bend as you work, and you'll want to have a fresh one handy.

For one project in this book, the guitar strap, which has leather ends, I suggest using a wedge-point needle, size 14–16. The wedge point is designed especially for use on leather.

Thread: All-purpose polyester or poly/cotton thread is appropriate for all the projects in this book.

Maintenance: The internal workings of a sewing machine have to be maintained. The moving parts must be oiled from time to time, but only with the tiniest amount of very lightweight sewing-machine oil. Extra oil will show up on your fabric, and heavy oil that was not produced specifically for sewing machines will become gummy.

Read your sewing machine manual carefully to find out where each drop of oil should be applied. Use the special long-nosed oil dropper that came with your machine. It will allow you to aim each tiny drop of oil in the exact location.

Lint fibers from your fabric will collect in the bobbin case of your machine over time and must be removed. If they are allowed to build up, they can jam the works, particularly if they absorb excess oil and become solid. Use a watercolor-type brush to dust all the surfaces and moving parts in and around the bobbin case periodically. Your machine's manual will tell you how to remove the bobbin case for cleaning.

A FEW THOUGHTS

You don't need tons of space and state-of-the-art equipment to enjoy sewing. I live in a little New York apartment, have a tiny cubby for my sewing space, and have sewn all sorts of projects, big and small. You can do the same. Keep the space neat, the surfaces cleared, and your tools put away, and guess what—you can make it work.

My cubby

Bandana-rama—Wrap, Glue, Sew

Index of Sewing Techniques

Throughout this book, you will have the chance to try new techniques.

Some of the techniques are described in Sewing Basics (page 20) and other techniques relating specifically to a project are included in the project instructions. If you want to review any of the techniques, refer back to this index for the page number.

Sewing Basics

Sewing is a wonderfully creative process

from your first concept of what you want to make, to thinking about colors and patterns, to actually putting the pieces together and making something of your own design and artistry.

However, creativity, whether in sewing or any other craft, requires knowing and respecting the process to achieve the best results. In other words, there are rules to follow. Even a simple seam in sewing has several steps.

READY, GET KNOTTED, SEW!

Before you start sewing, you have to thread a needle and make a knot in the end—then you're off and running.

Most hand sewing is done with a single strand of thread. That means when you thread the needle, you make a knot at only one end of the strand. The other end stays free so that you can adjust the length of the strand as you stitch. Keep the length of the thread fairly short (no more than about 15″) so that it doesn't tangle as you work.

TIP

If you have trouble threading the needle, give the end of the thread a fresh cut with sharp scissors and try again.

Sewist's Knot

There's a knack to making a knot at the end of a thread by rolling a twist off the tip of your index finger. It is a special trick known to sewists, and now you're one of them!

1. Wrap the end of the thread around the tip of your index finger.

2. Press your index finger and thumb together. Roll the wrapped thread off the fingertip by sliding the index finger toward the hand.

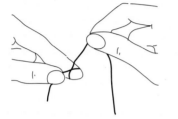

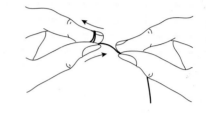

3. Pull the rolled knot in the thread gently toward the end of the strand, using your index finger and thumb. It will form a tight knot.

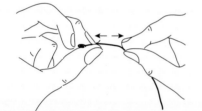

TIPS

If your knot doesn't appear the first time, keep trying. All of a sudden, you will get the hang of it, and knotting will be a cinch from then on.

I find it helps to have my thumb and index finger slightly damp when I make this knot.

Running Stitch

This is the simplest hand stitch there is, but you will find many ways to use it. For basting seams and gathering fabric, use a long running stitch.

1. Thread the needle and knot the thread.

2. Working from right to left (left-handers should do the opposite), dip the needle in and out of the fabric several times. Make the stitches and the spaces between them about ¼″ in length.

3. Pull the thread through. Repeat until you complete the line of stitching.

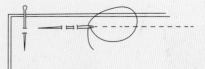

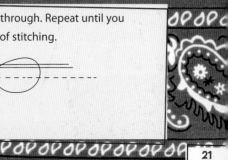

Finishing Knot

You will need to tie a finishing knot at the end of a line of hand stitching to keep the stitches in place.

1. Dip the needle down through the fabric and then back up again, pulling the thread to leave a small loop on the top.

2. Make a small stitch behind the loop, and then pass the needle through the loop and pull the thread tight.

3. Repeat for an extra-secure knot. Trim the thread.

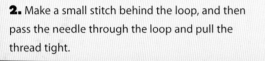

Sewing Seams by Machine

For perfect results, pinning and pressing are just as important as stitching the seam.

Take your time. Follow the steps, one at a time. No rush. After you learn the rules and don't have to think about them, your creativity can run free—and you'll be so proud of what you can do.

1. Place 2 pieces of fabric right sides together and align the 2 edges for the seam.

2. Pin or baste (hand stitch) the edges together.

3. Sew the seam with the proper seam allowance or seam width. The projects will tell you how wide to make the seam.

4. Lock in the stitches at the start and finish of a seam to prevent it from coming undone. To do this, make a few stitches forward and press the forward–reverse control to go back over the first stitches. Release the control, stitch forward to the end of the seam, and repeat.

5. Press the seam open.

1 Getting a Head Start:
Rose, Headbands, and Bow

There's more than one way to top off an outfit with a bright bandana.

Try these fresh takes on a classic look.

Things You'll Need

- ☐ Steam iron
- ☐ Yardstick
- ☐ Chalk pencil
- ☐ Sewing or pinking shears
- ☐ Needle and thread
- ☐ Glue gun
- ☐ Thimble *(optional)*

Bandana Rose

If you can cut a strip of fabric and sew a running stitch, you can make a bandana rose. Who knew a rose could be so versatile? Trim a hat or a headband, pin a rose on your lapel, or sew one onto your sneakers in as many colors as you like.

MAKE THE ROSE

▶**1**. Iron the bandana and lay it flat. Decide what section of the bandana to use. A strip cut along the hemmed edge will create a solid-color rose. A strip cut from the paisley border will create a richly patterned rose.

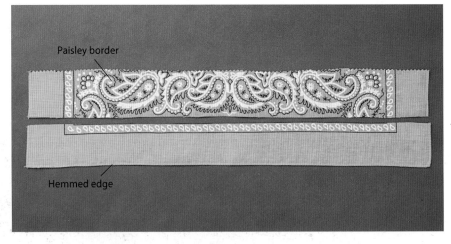

Paisley border

Hemmed edge

▶**2**. Use the yardstick and chalk pencil to draw the cutting line parallel to the edge of the bandana. A strip approximately 2″–2¼″ wide across the full width of the bandana is perfect. Cut along the cutting line. (Use pinking shears for more decorative "petals.")

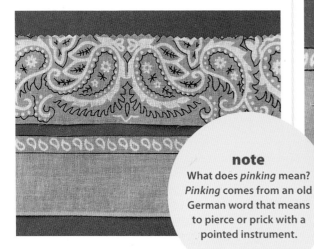

note
What does *pinking* mean? *Pinking* comes from an old German word that means to pierce or prick with a pointed instrument.

▶**3**. Thread the needle and knot the end. Sew a running stitch (page 21) about ¼″ from 1 long edge of the strip.

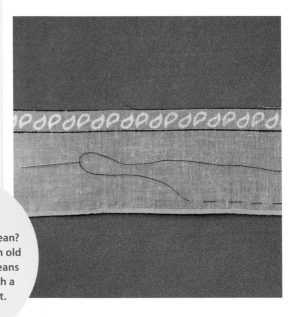

▶**4**. As you near the end and you start running out of thread, slide the fabric gently toward the knotted end. The fabric will gather and curl in on itself.

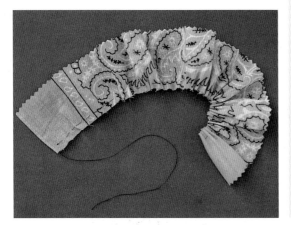

▶**5**. When you reach the end of the strip, set the needle down. Pick up the strip, and finish sliding the fabric toward the knot. Beginning at the knotted end, wrap the gathered edge tightly around itself to form the rose.

▶**6**. Hold the rose by the gathered edge. Pick up the needle and push it through the gathered layers to hold the bottom of the rose together. Use a thimble if it's helpful. Push the needle through the layers again in the opposite direction. Repeat this step if necessary to secure the gathers.

▶**7**. Secure the stitches with a finishing knot. Trim off the excess thread and—ta-da!—you have a rose. Adjust the petals and carefully attach the rose to a hat—or whatever you like—with a dab of hot glue from the glue gun.

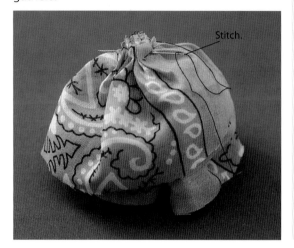

Stitch.

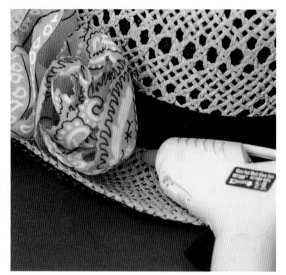

▶**8**. Add as many roses as you want in as many colors as you like.

note
What's the difference between scissors and shears? Though scissors and shears are used for similar purposes, dressmaking shears are designed with a bent handle to make it easier to cut fabric on a tabletop. Most shears have one handle-loop large enough to accommodate 3 or 4 fingers. Reserve your sewing scissors and shears for use on fabric only. Cutting paper can make scissors dull. Keep another pair of scissors for paper crafts.

BANDANA COUNT:

1

is enough to cover 1 or 2 headbands.

Things You'll Need

- [ ] Plastic headband
- [ ] Measuring tape
- [ ] Sewing scissors
- [ ] White craft glue
- [ ] Watercolor brush
- [ ] Water for rinsing the brush
- [ ] Glue gun
- [ ] Piece of ½″-wide lace *(optional)*
- [ ] Bandana rose or bow *(optional)*

Smooth Headband

What does it take to give a plain plastic headband a fresh designer look? Just scissors, glue, and a bandana, of course! Start from scratch with a plain headband, available at sewing and craft stores, or pull the fabric off an old headband and give it a new life. Either way, this project takes only a few minutes. Give a little thought to what section of the bandana you want to use before you cut into it.

MAKE THE HEADBAND

▶ **1**. Measure the headband and cut a bandana strip about 1″ longer than the headband and twice as wide as the widest section of the headband.

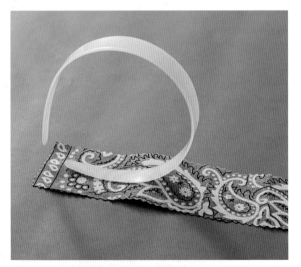

Smooth Headband

▶**2**. Drizzle white glue over the outer curve of the headband. Use the brush to spread the glue. The glue should cover the outer curve of the headband in a thin coating that will not ooze through the fabric.

TIP

If glue bleeds through the bandana in spots, don't panic! When the glue dries, rub the spots with a lightly moistened cloth and allow them to dry.

▶**3**. Center the cut strip of bandana on the glued side of the headband. Smooth the fabric with your fingers, starting at the top and working your way down each side. The strip should extend ½″ beyond each tip of the headband.

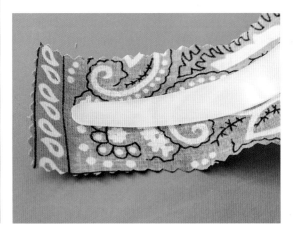

▶**4**. Brush a small amount of glue on the inside of the headband tips. Fold the extra ½″ at 1 end of the bandana strip to the inside and press it smoothly into place. Repeat at the other end. Allow the glue to set for a few minutes.

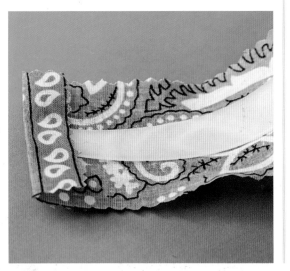

▶**5**. Trim the edges of the bandana strip with scissors so that they just meet or overlap slightly when you fold them to the inside of the headband.

▶**6**. Brush a thin coating of white glue over the inside surface of the headband. Fold the edges of the strip in, 1 side at a time, and press them into place.

▶ **7**. *Optional:* If you want to cover the raw edges of the fabric on the inside of the headband, cut a strip of lace the length of the headband. Brush white glue over the raw edges. Press the lace into place, smoothing it with your fingers. Allow it to dry thoroughly. Rinse the brush well in cool water.

▶ **8**. Wear the headband as is, or trim it with a fabric bow, a bandana rose (page 24), or a bunny bow (page 35), mixing or matching colors as you like. Attach the trims carefully with a dab of hot glue.

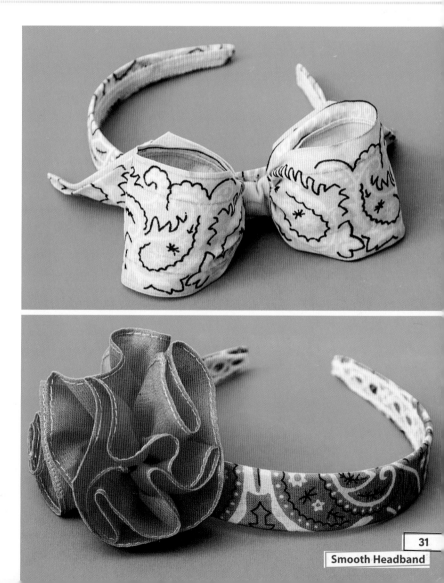

Things You'll Need

- [ ] Steam iron
- [ ] Yardstick
- [ ] Chalk pencil
- [ ] Sewing scissors
- [ ] Plastic headband
- [ ] White craft glue
- [ ] Watercolor brush
- [ ] Water for rinsing
      the brush

Wrapped Headband

*This headband goes together in minutes. When it's done,
it will look as if you simply twisted a bandana and tied it
around your hair. The bandana is cut on the bias (diagonally)
to give each strip a little stretch for a smooth wrap.*

MAKE THE HEADBAND

▶ **1**. Press the bandana and lay it flat. With the yardstick and chalk pencil, mark a 2½"- to 3"-wide strip at the center of the bandana, working from 1 corner of the square to the opposite. Cut out the strip.

▶ **2**. With the iron on the cotton setting but the steam turned off, press each long edge of the strip toward the middle, so that the strip is about 1½" wide. Set the strip aside.

Fold.

Fold.

Wrapped Headband

3. Cut 2 small rectangles of bandana, each about 1″ × 2″, from a bandana piece left over from Step 1. Brush white glue over the inner and outer surfaces of the headband tips. Fold 1 of the small pieces of bandana over each tip. Fold in the sides and glue into place.

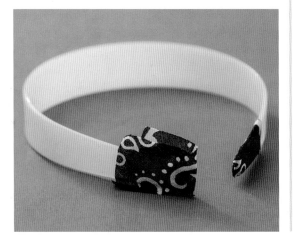

4. Squeeze a dot of white glue on the lower inside edge at 1 end of the headband. Holding the long strip from Step 2 angled toward the top of the headband, press the end firmly into the dot of glue. Begin wrapping the headband, allowing the wraps to overlap slightly. Put a dot of glue on the band under each round to prevent the wraps from shifting.

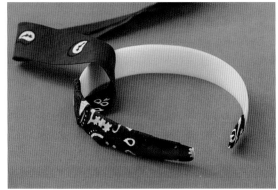

5. Complete the wrapping, ending on the inside of the headband. Trim the strip with scissors and glue the end in place. Allow the glue to dry.

6. Wear the headband as is or add a fabric bow, a couple of bandana roses (page 24), or another trim.

Bunny Bow

The casually tied Bunny Bow is popping up in fashion shoots everywhere. Make one bow, and presto chango, you can attach it to any headband and remove it again.

BANDANA COUNT:

1

(or the 2 leftover corner scraps from the Wrapped Headband, page 32)

Things You'll Need

MAKE THE BOW

☐ Steam iron

☐ Ruler

☐ Chalk pencil

☐ Scissors

☐ Dressmaker's pins

☐ Sewing machine or needle and thread

▶ **1.** Press the bandana and lay it flat. Measure 10″ from a corner along 1 edge and make a chalk mark. From the same corner, measure 10″ along the other edge and make a chalk mark. Draw a line connecting the 2 marks to make a triangle. Cut along the diagonal. Repeat to cut a second triangle from the opposite corner.

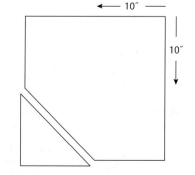

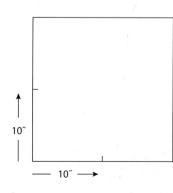

Bandana-rama—Wrap, Glue, Sew

2. Line up the 2 triangles with the right sides together. Pin them along the long edge. Using the machine or a needle and thread, sew the 2 pieces together, ½″ from the long edge. If you are hand sewing, use the running stitch (page 21) but make the stitches and the spaces between them ⅛″ long instead of ¼″.

3. Press the seam open (see Sewing Seams by Machine, page 22). Trim the corners of the seam, as shown. When you turn the piece to the right side, it will look like a mini bandana about 9½″ square with 4 hemmed edges.

Trim.

Trim.

4. With the right side facing down, fold the 2 seamed corners in toward the center of the square and press (A). Fold each side in half again (B). Fold the strip in half for the last time (C).

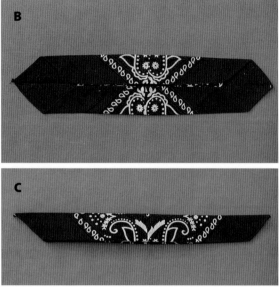

B

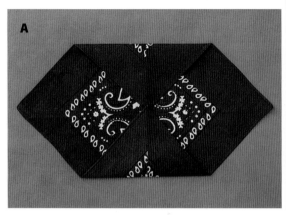

A

C

5. Wrap the strip around the headband and tie it once.

Bangles and Bows

Do you have an old bangle bracelet that needs a makeover? Follow the instructions for the Smooth Headband (page 28) or the Wrapped Headband (page 32) and give your bangle a bandana treatment. Then add your favorite trims for a totally new look. I found this bangle for a dollar in a thrift shop and transformed it with wrapping and a bunny bow.

2 Tweak Your Wardrobe:
Belt, Hoodie, and Shorts

Sometimes little things make all the difference. Make an eye-catching belt or add a bandana accent to your old hoodie or jean shorts for a quick wardrobe makeover.

Things You'll Need

- [ ] Measuring tape
- [ ] Pencil and paper
- [ ] Steam iron
- [ ] Sewing scissors or pinking shears
- [ ] Dressmaker's pins
- [ ] Sewing machine
- [ ] 2 D-rings (or circular binder rings), 1½″ diameter
- [ ] Needle and thread
- [ ] Lightweight fusible interfacing (optional)
- [ ] Turning tool (optional)

Two-Color Ring Belt

The D-ring belt is a classic, but this one has the surprise element of changing color halfway around, adding a double splash of color to your look. The belt is also super easy to put together. Keep this in mind at holiday time, and make belts for your besties in their favorite shades.

MAKE THE BELT

▶ **1.** Try on your favorite pair of pants. Measure around the top of your pants while you are wearing them. Write down the measurement.

▶ **2.** To get the colors to change at the center back, the tail side of the belt must be longer than the ring side. Take the measurement you wrote down in Step 1 and divide it in half. Add 7″ to that number for the tail side and 2″ to that number for the ring side.

Tail side

Ring side

▶ **3.** Press the bandanas and cut a 4½″-wide strip from each. Trim 1 strip to the length you determined for the tail side and the other to the length for the ring side. Pin the 2 pieces together at 1 end with the right sides together. Sew the seam using the machine, leaving a ½″ seam allowance. Press the seam open (see Sewing Seams by Machine, page 22).

Two-Color Ring Belt

Slipstitch

Mastering a basic hemming stitch gives you wardrobe freedom. With that little bit of knowledge, you can shorten a skirt, repair a hem, and tweak your wardrobe by customizing your favorite clothes. Having things exactly the way you want them—when you want them—ah!

A number of different methods can be used for hemming, all with slightly different purposes. The one I find the most useful is called the slipstitch. I like it because it's almost invisible, it's sturdy, it's quick, and it's handy for other little sewing jobs too.

1. Fold the hem to the desired depth. If the hem has a raw (cut) edge, turn the edge under ½″. Pin the hem into place.

2. Thread a needle and knot an end of the thread.

3. Working from right to left (left-handers should do the opposite), push the needle through the edge of the hem, make the tiniest stitch in the main fabric, and then go back into the hem about ¼″ away. Pull the thread through and repeat. Easy.

4. Cut a piece of interfacing to correspond with the length and width of the belt from Step 3. Iron the interfacing to the wrong side of the belt, following the manufacturer's directions.

note
Step 4 is optional. You can make the belt without interfacing, but fusible (iron-on) interfacing will give the belt a nice weight and feel. It will also keep the fabric from wrinkling each time you wear it.

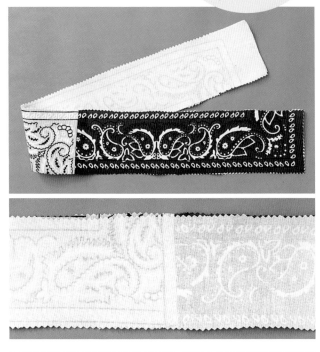

5. Fold the strip in half lengthwise with the right sides together. Pin the strip along the open edge and then sew the long edges together, leaving a ¼″ allowance. Stop 1½″ before you reach the end of the belt.

note
Here is where you get to use the sewing machine's handwheel to create an angle in the seam. The handwheel is located on the upper right side of the machine. When you come to a halt in the seam (Step 5), turn the wheel toward yourself so that the needle is fully inserted in the fabric. Now lift the presser foot lever to raise the foot, and turn the fabric so that the stitching will be aimed toward the bottom corner of the belt (Step 6).

6. Lower the presser foot again and sew, allowing the stitches to run off the edge. Trim the extra fabric from the point.

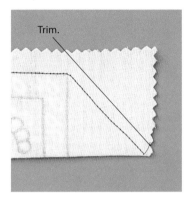

7. To turn the belt right side out, begin by folding back the fabric at the opening of the belt. Dampen your index finger and place it inside the belt opening. Draw the inside of the belt to the outside, by sliding your index finger against your thumb.

8. If needed, insert a turning tool to gently press out the seams of the angled end. Remove the tool and iron the belt.

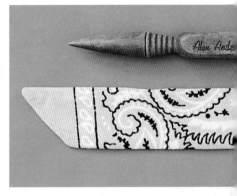

9. Slip the squared end of the belt though the 2 D-rings. Fold the end under ½″ and pin. Use the needle and thread to stitch a mini hem (see Slipstitch, page 42) to secure the rings in place.

10. Fasten the belt by inserting the tail end through both rings, from bottom to top. Then fold the tail over the top ring and under the bottom ring. Pull it through snugly.

Things You'll Need

- ☐ Steam iron
- ☐ Large piece of paper (such as the back of a piece of wrapping paper)
- ☐ Pencil
- ☐ Scissors
- ☐ Dressmaker's pins
- ☐ Sewing machine
- ☐ Needle and thread

Lined Hoodie

It's amazing what a little burst of color can do. I love the way the contrasting bandana lining adds so much style to this simple hoodie. Adding the lining will make good use of your new hemming skills too. It's sewn in by hand, but even so, the entire project from start to finish takes only about an hour.

MAKE THE LINING

▷ **1**. Press the bandana. Fold it in half, carefully matching the printed borders. Press the fold and set the bandana aside.

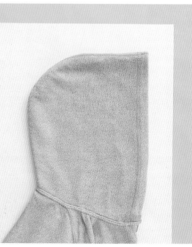

▷ **2**. Place a large sheet of paper on your work surface. Fold the sweatshirt's hood smoothly along the seamline and center it on the sheet of paper. Use the pencil to trace the outer edge of the hood. This will be the pattern for the lining.

Lined Hoodie

3. Set the hoodie aside and cut out the paper pattern, staying ½″ outside the tracing line, all the way around. Pin the pattern to the folded bandana, lining up the front-opening edge with the hemmed edge of the bandana.

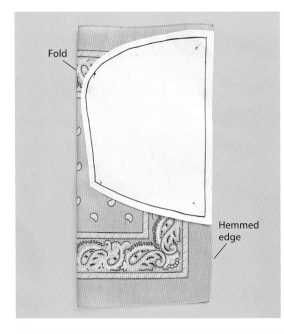

4. Cut the bandana along the edge of the pattern and then remove the pattern. Place the 2 halves of the lining with their right sides together and pin along the top and back edges. On the machine, stitch the 2 halves together along the top and back.

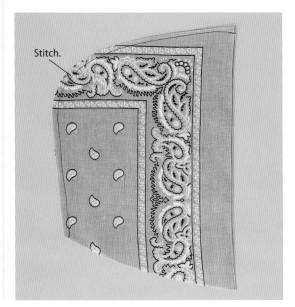

5. Press the seam open. If the fabric wrinkles over the curve, don't worry. The wrinkles will disappear when you wear the hood. Turn the front and bottom edges of the lining under ½″ (toward the wrong side) and press.

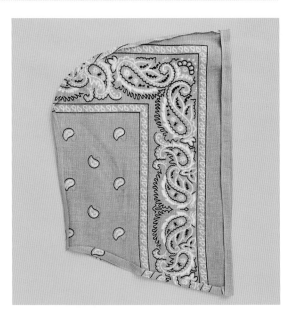

▶ **6**. Turn the sweatshirt hood wrong side out. Arrange the lining over the hood, with the wrong sides together. Pin the lining into place along the hemmed edge of the hood's front opening and along the neck seam.

▶ **7**. With the needle and thread, hem the lining into place along the pinned edges. Use the slipstitch (page 42), making the stitches tiny and even and no more than ¼″ apart so that they are barely visible.

note
If my reminders to make the stitches "small and even" seem a little tiresome, you won't think so when you look at your finished project. Careful craftsmanship pays off in the end. You'll be so proud of yourself and your work when it looks like it came from a designer shop.

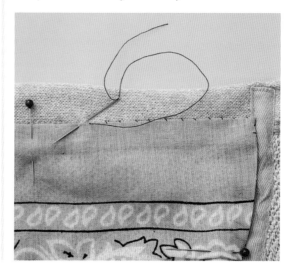

▶ **8**. On the inside of the hood, attach the bandana lining to the sweatshirt by taking 2 small stitches at the top of the back seam. Tie a finishing knot (page 22) to hold the stitches in place. These little stitches will ensure that the lining does not come loose when you pull the hood on and off.

Bandana-Trimmed Shorts

Change the look of your shorts without changing the length. Choose a fresh, bright bandana border in a color that works with your favorite tops.

Things You'll Need

- ☐ Measuring tape
- ☐ Paper and pencil
- ☐ Steam iron
- ☐ Yardstick
- ☐ Chalk pencil
- ☐ Sewing scissors
- ☐ Sewing machine
- ☐ Dressmaker's pins
- ☐ Needle and thread

TRIM THE SHORTS

▶**1**. You'll need 2 identical bandana strips to make the borders. Start with a little easy bandana math to determine their width and length. Lay the shorts flat on your work surface. Decide how deep you want the finished border to be. (The depth of the border on the shorts shown here is 1¼˝.) Double that number and add 1˝. (This will be the width of each strip.) Measure across the hem on 1 leg of the shorts. Double that number and add 1˝. (This will be the length of each strip.)

▶**2**. Press the bandana and lay it flat. Use the yardstick and chalk pencil to mark 2 matching sections of the bandana, using the measurements from Step 1. Cut out the 2 strips.

▶**3**. Fold a strip in half crosswise, with the right sides together. Pin; then sew the side seam, leaving a ½˝ seam allowance. Repeat with the second strip.

▶**4**. Press each seam open. Fold under the top and bottom edges ½˝ toward the wrong side and press.

49

5. Slip a bandana border over 1 of the leg openings, with the right sides of the bandana and the shorts together. Open the bottom fold of the border toward the hem of the shorts. The measurement from the fold line to the hemline should be the same as the depth you measured in Step 1. (In the pictures shown here, it is 1¼˝.) Pin the bandana strip into place.

6. On the machine, sew along the fold line around the leg of the shorts.

Stitch.

7. Remove the pins and turn the border strip so that it hangs below the hem of the shorts.

8. Fold the border to the inside of the leg and pin it into place. Be sure the ½˝ fold on the inside is turned under. The depth of the border should be the same on the inside as it is on the outside.

9. With the needle and thread, hand stitch the border on the inside of the leg, using the slipstitch (page 42). Repeat Steps 5–9 with the second leg, and you're good to go.

3 Gatherings:
Top and Skirts

Sewing a channel, or casing, allows you to gather fabric with elastic or a drawstring.
Casings are used in waistbands, gathered sleeves, and duffel bags. Each of the three
projects in this chapter makes use of a variation of a fold-over casing.

Drawstring Top

Making a top doesn't get any easier than this. By folding over the edge of a bandana and sewing the fold into place, you create a casing. Simply thread a ribbon through the casing to gather the fabric for the look and fit you want. The more this top is washed, the softer the gathers will be.

Things You'll Need

- ☐ Steam iron
- ☐ Dressmaker's pins
- ☐ Sewing machine
- ☐ 2 yards of 1″-wide ribbon
- ☐ Safety pin

MAKE THE TOP

1. Press a bandana and lay it flat, wrong side up. Fold 1 edge along the outer line of the paisley border. Press the fold.

2. Turn the hemmed edge of the fold under so the casing is about 1⅛″ wide. Pin and then sew the casing on the machine, as close to the edge as possible. Repeat with the second bandana.

3. Cut the ribbon in half. Attach a safety pin to the end of 1 piece.

4. Slide the safety pin into the end of a casing and work it through to the other end. Push the fabric over the head of the safety pin with 1 hand and draw the fabric away from the pin with the other. Repeat with the second bandana and yard of ribbon.

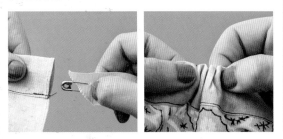

5. Lay the 2 bandanas flat with their wrong sides together. Tie the ribbons at each shoulder.

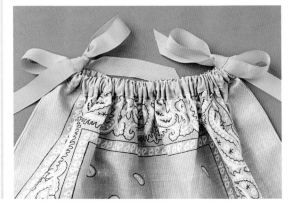

6. Slip the top over your head. Retie the ribbons if necessary over your shoulders. Adjust the folds of the fabric and the length of the ribbons to fit.

7. Bring the front and the back of the top together under 1 arm. Determine where you want the underarm seam to begin and mark the spot with a pin. Repeat on the other side. Carefully remove the top.

8. Turn the top inside out. Line up the side edges and pin each side from the underarm to the bottom edge. Sew the side seams, leaving a ½˝ seam allowance.

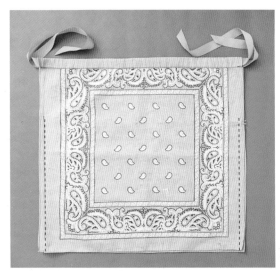

9. Press the seams open, turn the top right side out, and you're all set.

Ribbon Dirndl Skirt

This cute skirt is basically two bandanas sewn together with seams at center front and center back. Bandana fabric is so lightweight that a skirt made from the fabric has to be lined. Because of the way this skirt is put together, I've treated the bandanas and their linings as if they were a single piece of fabric.

A ribbon threaded through a casing at the top of the skirt creates the gathered waist. This type of casing has a header, an extra fold of fabric above the casing that forms a ruffle. The casing for this skirt begins and ends at either side of the front opening, so the ribbon is tied at the center front.

Things You'll Need

- ☐ 1 yard cotton batiste or other lightweight lining material
- ☐ Steam iron
- ☐ Dressmaker's pins
- ☐ Sewing scissors or pinking shears
- ☐ Needle and thread
- ☐ Sewing machine
- ☐ Yardstick
- ☐ Removable fabric marker
- ☐ Safety pin
- ☐ 1 to 1½ yards 1″-wide grosgrain ribbon
- ☐ Seam ripper

MAKE THE SKIRT

note
What's a dirndl? In some German dialects *dirndl* means "young girl" or "maid," but it also refers to a traditional dress with a gathered skirt and a tight, low-necked bodice.

▶ **1**. Lay the lining material flat on a work surface. Press a bandana and lay it on top of the lining, right side up. Pin it into place and cut the lining the same size as the bandana. Repeat with the second bandana.

▶ **2**. With the lining material pinned in place, baste the linings to the bandanas, close to the edges, using the needle and thread. Press the bandanas to make sure the 2 layers fit together smoothly, like a single piece of fabric. Remove the pins.

Bandana-rama—Wrap, Glue, Sew

3. Line up the bandanas with the right sides together. Decide which edge will form the back seam of the skirt. Make sure the border designs line up; then pin and sew the back seam on the sewing machine, leaving a ½˝ allowance. Press the seam open.

4. Pin the edges together for the skirt's front seam. Begin the seam 5˝ to 6˝ down from the top edge to allow for the front opening. Sew the seam, leaving a 1˝ seam allowance. Press the seam open.

5. Make the headed casing. Make a 2½˝ fold along the top edge of the skirt, folding toward the inside. Pin the fold into place. On the machine, sew along the bottom edge of the folded section, keeping your stitches on top of the bandana's prehemmed stitches.

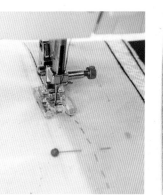

Headed Casing

1. Fold 1 edge of a bandana toward the wrong side of the fabric and press. (The depth of the fold will depend upon the width of your ribbon. A 2½˝ fold will work well for a 1˝-wide ribbon.)

2. Pin the fold into place. On the machine, sew along the pinned edge.

3. Using the width of the ribbon plus ¼˝ as a measurement, measure and mark a line above the first line of stitching. On the machine, sew along the marked line to divide the casing and heading.

▶ **6**. Measure and mark a line 1¼″ above the first line of stitching. Using the sewing machine, stitch along the marked line.

▶ **7**. Turn the skirt right side out. Attach a safety pin to the end of the ribbon and ease it through the casing.

▶ **8**. Try the skirt on. Adjust the ends of the ribbon so they are equal in length and tie a bow. Adjust the gathers of the skirt evenly around your waist.

▶ **9**. Determine the length you would like the skirt to be. Mark the length with pins. Fold the lower edge to the inside at the pins, and press. Sew the hem with the slipstitch (page 42). Use a seam ripper to pull out the lining's basting stitches if you wish.

Ruffled Miniskirt

I've given this fun mini a rating of "a little tricky." The tricky part comes with adding the ruffle—but that also adds the fun. Have someone with experience help you with gathering and stitching the ruffle onto the skirt. The rest—including the lining and casing—you'll have no trouble doing yourself.

The lining has only one seam—a French seam. This type of double-sewn seam encloses the raw edges of the fabric inside it. The double sewing prevents the fabric from fraying and leaves you with a very finished, professional look.

Things You'll Need

- [ ] Steam iron
- [ ] Sewing scissors or pinking shears
- [ ] 1 yard lightweight cotton fabric (at least 45″ wide) for lining
- [ ] Dressmaker's pins
- [ ] Sewing machine
- [ ] Yardstick
- [ ] Chalk pencil
- [ ] Measuring tape
- [ ] ¾″-wide no-roll elastic
- [ ] Safety pin
- [ ] Seam ripper
- [ ] Needle and thread

MAKE THE MINI

Start with the Lining ▷▷▷

▶**1.** Fold the lining material in half on your work surface. The fold will be the center front of the lining. Lay a bandana on top of the lining with 1 edge lined up along the fold. Pin the bandana into place, cut out the lining along the 3 unfolded edges, and remove the bandana.

▶**2.** The edges opposite the fold will be the center back seam of the lining. Follow the directions in French Seam (page 61). Set the lining aside.

Bandana-rama—Wrap, Glue, Sew

Make the Skirt ▷▷▷

1. Press the bandanas and set aside 2 of them for the ruffle. Take the 2 bandanas for the skirt section and trim off 1 plain border (about 1¾″) from each. The trimmed sides will be the top edge of the skirt.

2. Line up the 2 skirt pieces with the right sides together and the trimmed edges at the top. Pin the side seams. Sew the side seams on the machine with a ½″ allowance. Press the seams open. Turn the skirt right side out.

3. Lay the skirt flat. Using the yardstick and chalk pencil, measure and draw a line parallel to and 8″ above the bottom hemline. Turn the skirt over and repeat.

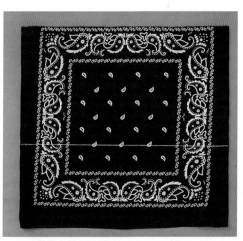

French Seam

1. Line up and pin the 2 edges for the seam with the wrong sides together.

2. Stitch the seam on the sewing machine with a ¼″ seam allowance. Trim the seam allowance to ⅛″, as shown.

Right side

3. Turn the lining inside out and press the seam flat to the side. Then fold the seam along the stitching line and press.

4. Sew the seam again, this time on the wrong side of the fabric, with a ¼″ allowance enclosing the raw edges.

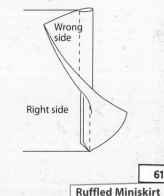

Wrong side

Right side

Gathered Ruffle

A ruffle is made by gathering a strip of fabric. The same technique can be used to make a puff sleeve or the waistband of a skirt.

1. Set the stitch gauge on the sewing machine to the longest setting. (Long stitches gather easily; short stitches do not.)

2. Sew 2 rows of stitching along the edge of a strip of fabric. The first line of stitching should be about ¼" from the edge. The second line of stitching should be ⅛" from the first. Allow the stitches to run off the ends of the strips and leave the threads long enough to hold on to.

3. Gently pull on the bobbin threads on the underside of the fabric to gather the fabric. Work from each end of the strip, pushing the gathers toward the center, until the gathers are even and the ruffle is the desired length. Pin in place.

Add the Ruffle ▷▷▷

▶**1**. Lay out the first of the reserved bandanas. Trim off the borders from 2 sides to make strips about 6″ wide and 22″ long. Repeat with the second bandana.

▶**2**. Line up 2 of the borders with the right sides together. Pin and sew a seam across 1 end to make a strip about 6″ × 44″. Press the seam open. Repeat with the second set of borders.

▶**3**. Have someone with experience help you with the next few steps. See Gathered Ruffle (at left) for guidance. Sew 2 rows of stitching along the top (cut) edge of a long strip. Repeat with the second long strip.

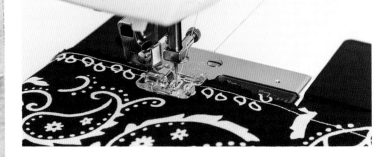

▶**4**. Select a strip. Gently pull on the bobbin threads to gather the fabric until the ruffle is the width of the skirt. Repeat with the second strip.

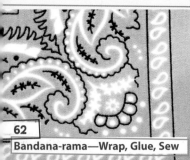

5. With the right sides of the ruffle and skirt front together and the hem of the ruffle facing the top of the skirt, pin the gathered edge of 1 ruffle along the chalk line on the skirt.

6. Repeat with the second ruffle on the back of the skirt. Allow the ruffles to overlap slightly at the side seams. Hand baste the ruffles into place (see Running Stitch, page 21) and remove the pins.

7. Set the stitch gauge on the machine back to the normal setting. Follow the basting stitches with a row of machine stitches, close to the gathered edge of the ruffle, all the way around the skirt. Make a second round of machine stitches, ¼″ away from the first, so that the ruffle is attached with 2 rows of stitching.

8. Flip the ruffle down so that it hangs toward the hem of the skirt. It will make a full, bouncy ruffle all the way around. Pick out any visible basting or gathering stitches with a seam ripper.

9. Slip the lining inside the skirt with the wrong sides together and the lining seam at center back. Line up the raw edges around the waistline, pin, and then baste the lining to the skirt all the way around. Remove the pins.

Fold-Down Casing

The gathered waist of this skirt is made with elastic and a fold-down casing. A simple fold-down casing is made in the same way as the headed casing (page 57) but without the extra ruffle at the top.

1. Fold down the top edge of the fabric ¼″ toward the wrong side, and press the fold.

2. Fold the edge again to the width of the elastic plus ¼″.

3. Pin the fold in place, leaving a 2″ opening. (This is where the elastic will be inserted.)

4. On the machine, sew the casing, ⅛″ from the pinned edge, leaving the 2″ opening free.

2″ opening

5. Sew the top edge of the casing, ⅛″ from the top fold.

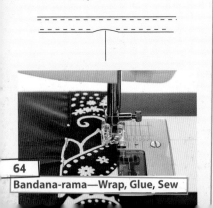

Make the Waistband ▷▷▷

▷ **1.** Follow the directions for the fold-down casing (at left). If your elastic is 1″ wide, make the fold for the casing 1¼″ deep.

▷ **2.** Center the 2″ opening in the casing over the center back seam in the lining.

▷ **3.** Measure your waist for a fit that is comfortable. Add 1″ to that measurement and cut a piece of elastic to that length. Attach a safety pin to the end of the elastic and ease it through the waistband casing.

▷ **4.** Overlap the ends of the elastic about ½″, and pin. Stitch the overlapped edges of the elastic together. Sew up the opening in the waistband casing by hand or on the machine.

▷ **5.** Try the skirt on. Turn under the raw edge of the lining at the hem ¼″, and then fold it again so that the length of the lining corresponds with the length of the skirt. Sew the lining hem with the slipstitch (page 42).

4 **Beautiful Borders:**
Tops and Bag

Pair up the paisley borders of bandanas to make bold, new patterns of your own.

LEVEL:
Medium

BANDANA COUNT:
4

Things You'll Need

- ☐ Steam iron
- ☐ Dressmaker's pins
- ☐ Needle
- ☐ Thread in a contrasting color
- ☐ Thread to match the bandanas
- ☐ Sewing scissors
- ☐ Sewing machine
- ☐ Seam ripper

Kimono-Sleeve Top

With its loose sleeves and off-the-shoulder ease, the Kimono-Sleeve Top is just the kind of light, fluttery top you'll want to reach for on a hot summer day. Wear it over your tank top or tankini and let the breezes carry you away.

note

A bandana's narrowly hemmed edges are the key to putting this blouse together. Since each of the four bandanas is used whole, there are no raw edges and no need for ½˝ seam allowances. Instead, to make the seams, overlap the hemmed edges by just the tiniest amount; then pin and hand baste before stitching on the machine.

MAKE THE TOP

▶ **1**. Press the bandanas and set 2 aside for the sleeves. Place the remaining 2 bandanas right side up on a work surface. Overlap the edges slightly and pin together, about 3˝ in at each end, to make the shoulders. The edges at each shoulder seam should not overlap more than ⅛˝ to ¼˝.

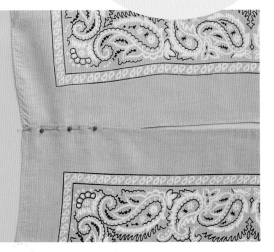

2. With a needle and contrasting-color thread, baste the 3″ seam at each end of the neck opening for the shoulders.

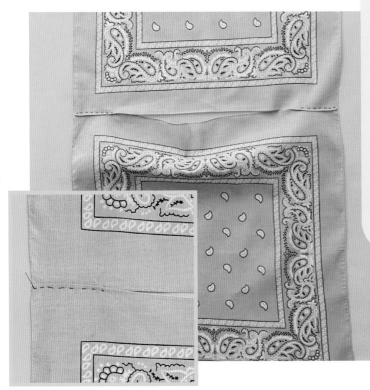

3. Stitch the shoulder seams on the sewing machine as shown, using matching thread and a short stitch. Try to stay in line with the bandana's rolled hem stitching so that the new stitches seem to disappear.

4. Remove the basting stitches from the shoulders with a seam ripper.

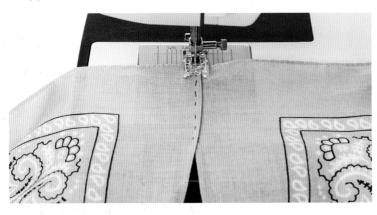

5. Lay the front and back of the top on your work surface, open as 1 long piece with the right side facing up. Select a bandana set aside in Step 1 as a sleeve. Lay it flat, centering 1 edge of the sleeve at the top's shoulder seam, overlapping the sleeve edge slightly. Pin and baste the overlapped edge of the sleeve into place.

6. Stitch the sleeve into place and remove the basting stitches, as with the shoulder seams in Steps 3 and 4.

7. Fold the sleeve in half as shown. Overlap the lower edges slightly, pin, and then baste the seam.

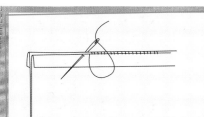

Overhand Stitch

The overhand stitch is used to join two folded or finished edges. You'll find many uses for it, beginning with these projects.

1. Hold the 2 edges together.

2. Working from right to left (left-handers do the opposite) and holding the needle at a diagonal, push the point of the needle from the back edge to the front edge. Insert the needle very close to the edges. Pull the thread through; then repeat to the end of the row. Tie off the thread with a finishing knot (page 22).

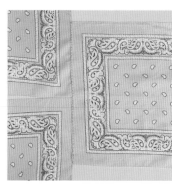

8. Stitch the underarm seam on the machine. Work slowly, easing the sleeve through as you stitch.

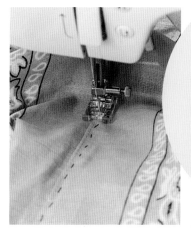

note

The sleeve is wide enough for you to sew all the way from wrist to underarm without stopping. However, you can also sew the seam in two steps. First, stitch from the wrist to the midpoint of the seam; then, turn the sleeve around and stitch from the underarm to the midpoint, overlapping the first set of stitches.

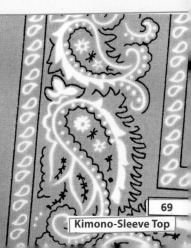

9. Remove the basting stitches with a seam ripper. Make a cuff by folding up the hem of the sleeve several times, and press.

10. Repeat Steps 5–9 with the second sleeve.

11. Line up the front and back along the side edges. Overlapping the edges slightly, pin and baste each seam below the arms, stopping 4˝ from the bottom. Stitch as before.

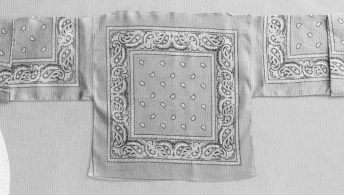

note
If you want to put your newfound hand-sewing skills to the test, you can make this summer cover-up entirely by hand while you sit by the pool. Follow the project directions, but instead of using the machine for the sewing, slipstitch (page 42) by hand or simply pin the hemmed edges and whip them together with tiny overhand stitches (page 69). I made a hand-sewn version of the blouse in about two hours.

Lined Pocket Shoulder Bag

I love this bag. The strap is wide enough for comfort on your shoulder, and the lined cotton has a wonderful feel. At 10″ deep and 11″ wide, it is big enough to carry a couple of books or a tablet, and the pockets are roomy enough for everything else.

MAKE THE BAG

▶ **1**. Select 1 of the main-color bandanas. Press the bandana and lay it flat on your work surface. On the left and right sides, trim off the outer borders to within ½″ of the paisley borders. Discard the trimmed borders.

▶ **2**. With the yardstick and chalk pencil, measure and draw a parallel line 6½″ from each trimmed edge. Cut along the chalk line on each side, and then cut each strip in half crosswise (A, B, C, and D), as shown. Set aside the center section (E) for the shoulder bag strap.

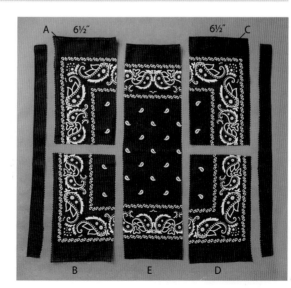

Bandana-rama—Wrap, Glue, Sew

3. Arrange pieces A and C from Step 2 as shown. Pin pieces A and C together with the right sides facing. On the sewing machine, stitch the sections together, leaving a ½″ seam allowance. Press the seam open. Repeat with pieces B and D.

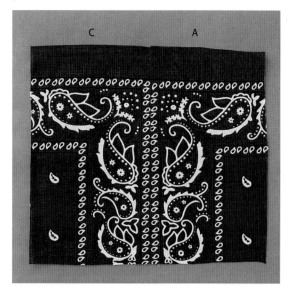

4. Press the second main-color bandana and cut it in half crosswise. Set aside 1 of the halves for another project. With the remaining half, trim each side, leaving ½″ outside the outer border. Draw a parallel line 6½″ from each trimmed edge and cut along the chalk lines. Place the 6½″-wide pieces right sides together and stitch, leaving a ½″ seam allowance. Press the seam open.

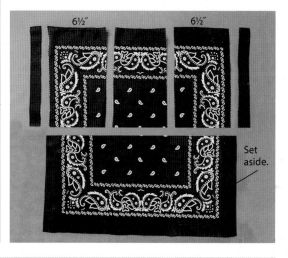

5. You now have 3 matching pieces: 2 for the front and back of the bag and 1 for the pocket section. Cut a piece of fusible interfacing for each of the 3 sections. Iron the interfacing onto the wrong side of each.

MAKE THE POCKET

1. Lay 2 of the pieces you've just completed on your work surface. You will use 1 for the pocket and the other for the front of the bag. Fold the plain border of the pocket to the wrong side and press the fold.

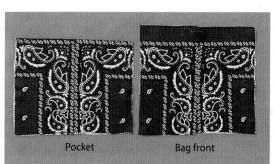

Pocket   Bag front

Squared Corners

Use the machine's handwheel to stitch crisp, square corners.

1. Line up the 2 layers of fabric and begin sewing at the top right corner.

2. Stitch along the right edge, leaving a ½″ seam allowance. Stop ½″ before you reach the lower edge.

3. Turn the handwheel toward yourself until the needle is fully inserted in the fabric.

4. Raise the lever to lift the presser foot, turn the fabric 90° counterclockwise, and then put the presser foot down again.

5. Sew across the bottom, leaving a ½″ seam allowance. Stop ½″ before you reach the left edge.

6. Repeat Steps 3 and 4.

7. Stitch along the left edge using a ½″ seam allowance. Continue sewing until you reach the top edge.

▶ **2.** Place the pocket on top of the front of the bag with the horizontal border of the pocket just below the wide horizontal border of the front. Trim off the section of the pocket that extends beyond the front. Pin the 2 pieces together along the center seam and the outer edges.

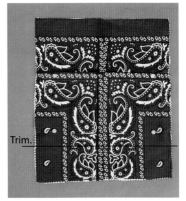

Trim.

▶ **3.** On the sewing machine, stitch the pocket to the front of the bag along the center seam as well as the left and right edges.

▶ **4.** Line up the front and back sections of the shoulder bag with the right sides together. Using the technique for making squared corners (at left), sew the side and bottom seams, leaving a ½″ seam allowance.

MAKE THE LINING

1. Press the bandana for the lining, fold it in half, and lay it flat on your work surface. With the bag still inside out, lay it on top of the lining material, centering it between the paisley borders and matching the hemmed edges at the top. Cut out the 2 pieces of lining along the side and bottom edges.

2. Line up the 2 lining pieces with the right sides together and the hemmed edges at the top. Use the machine to sew the left and right sides, leaving a ¼˝ seam allowance. Leave the top and bottom open. Set the lining aside.

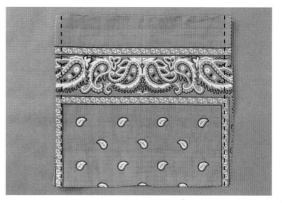

MAKE THE STRAP

1. Lay out the main-color strip of bandana (E) that you set aside in Make the Bag, Step 2 (page 71). Cut out a piece of fusible interfacing the same size and iron it onto the wrong side of the strip. Cut the strip in half lengthwise to make 2 pieces, each about 3˝ × 22˝. Cut 2 matching strips from the paisley borders of the remaining lining-color bandana.

2. With right sides together, sew the 2 main-color strips together end to end. Press the seam open. Repeat with the 2 lining strips.

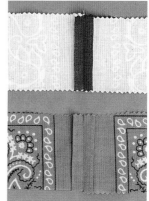

3. Line up the 2 long strips for the strap with right sides facing. Sew each long edge on the machine, leaving a ¼˝ seam allowance. Turn the strap right side out and press. See Two-Color Ring Belt, Step 7 (page 43) for tips on turning the strap right side out.

PUT IT ALL TOGETHER

▶**1**. Turn the bag right side out and press the seams.

▶**2**. Working at the top edge of the bag, center 1 end of the strap over a side seam, with the main colors facing. Pin it in place. Repeat with the other end of the strap and side seam, making sure the strap is not twisted. Check the strap for length and adjust it as needed. Stitch the ends of the strap in place on the machine, leaving a ¼″ seam allowance.

▶**3**. With the right side of the lining on the inside, slide it over the bag so the right sides are facing. Line up the top edges of the lining and bag, and pin together around the opening. On the machine, stitch the lining to the bag, about ¼″ down from the top edge, all the way around the opening.

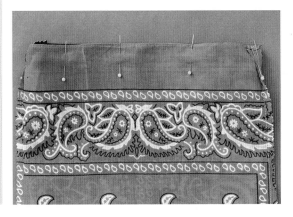

▶**4**. Pull the lining right side out, as shown, and press the seam around the opening.

▶**5**. Fold the lower edges of the lining under ½″ to the wrong side. Close the bottom seam of the lining using a neat, small overhand stitch (page 69).

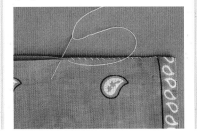

▶**6**. Tuck the lining inside, and you've got yourself a shoulder bag!

Yoked Tunic

Wear this tunic over leggings for a great summer look. If you haven't done a lot of sewing, I suggest working with someone with more experience the first time you try this project. Some fitting is involved in getting the straps positioned just right, and attaching the skirt to the yoked top (the horizontal band and shoulder straps) might be a little daunting the first time around.

BANDANA COUNT:

5

(2 of one color for the yoke, 3 for the skirt)

Things You'll Need

- ☐ Steam iron
- ☐ Sewing scissors or pinking shears
- ☐ Dressmaker's pins
- ☐ Chalk pencil
- ☐ Needle
- ☐ Matching thread and contrasting-color thread
- ☐ Seam ripper
- ☐ 4-foot length of narrow ribbon
- ☐ Beads or charms *(optional)*

MAKE THE YOKE

▶ **1**. Press a bandana and lay it flat. Cut 2 of the paisley borders (each about 4″ × 22″) for the horizontal band of the yoke.

4″

4″

Bandana-rama—Wrap, Glue, Sew

2. For the back band, trim off the plain borders (about 2½″) at each end of 1 strip. For the front band, cut the other strip in half crosswise.

3. Cut 2 strips, the same dimensions as the bands from Step 1, from the remaining piece of the bandana. These strips will be used as facings (linings) for the yoke.

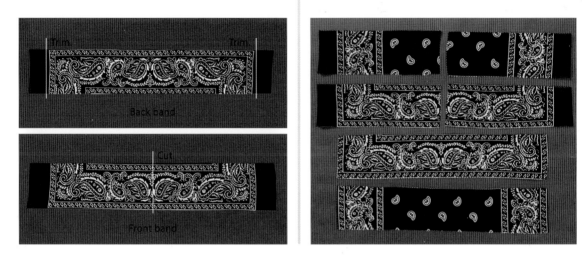

4. Line up the pieces for the horizontal band of the yoke, end to end. The 2 pieces for the front will join either end of the strip for the back, with the hemmed edges facing outward.

5. With the right sides together, sew the 3 pieces together to make 1 long strip. Repeat Steps 3 and 4 with the pieces for the horizontal-band facing.

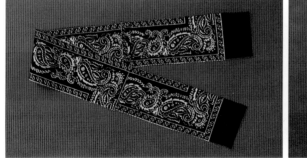
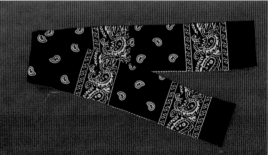

6. To cut out the straps, begin by pressing the second yoke bandana. Fold over 1 edge along the paisley border.

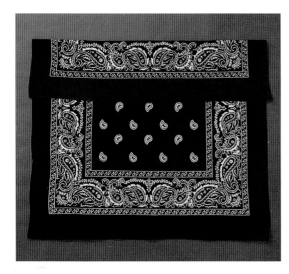

7. Cut through 2 layers along the outer paisley border (about a 3″ width). Repeat Steps 6 and 7 with the border on the opposite side for the second strap.

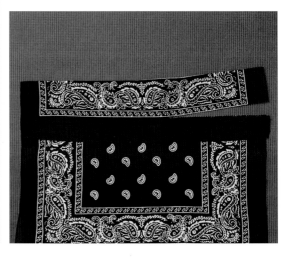

8. Fold the fabric for each strap lengthwise so that the right sides are together. Pin along the long edges and sew, using the paisley border as your sewing guide.

9. Turn the straps right side out and press.

10. Here is where you might want someone to help you. Wrap the horizontal band of the yoke around your chest, just below your arms. Pin the ends of the strip together at the center front; the fit should be comfortable and slightly loose. Then pin the straps into place. Mark the pinned spots with a chalk pencil, and then remove the pins.

11. Sew the straps into place, with the right sides of the straps facing the right side of the yoke. Trim the ends of the straps, if needed, leaving enough for a ½″ seam allowance on each end.

12. Lay out the yoke with the straps folded downward. Pin the facing into place along the top edge of the yoke, right sides together. (The straps will be sandwiched between the 2 layers.)

13. Sew the top edge and short center-front seams. Trim the seams, turn the yoke right side out, and press.

MAKE THE SKIRT

▶**1**. Line up the 3 bandanas for the skirt and pin them, with the right sides together, along the side edges. At the top edge of what will be the center-front seam, leave a 1½″–2″ opening.

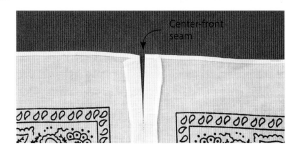

▶**2**. Sew the 3 seams, leaving a ½″ allowance, and press the seams open.

▶**3**. Have someone with experience help you with the following steps: making the gathers and joining the skirt to the yoke. See Gathered Ruffle (page 62) for details on gathering. With the machine's stitch gauge set for the longest stitch and the fabric right side up, sew 2 rows of gathering stitches along the top edge of the skirt. Leave the ends of the threads long when you remove the skirt from the sewing machine.

▶**4**. Gently pull the bobbin threads to gather the fabric. Work from either end, making even gathers all around.

PUT IT ALL TOGETHER

▶**1**. With the right sides together, pin the gathered edge of the skirt to the bottom of the yoke at the center front and the center back. Slide the ruffles so they are evenly spaced between the pins, adding more pins as needed. Be sure to pin the skirt to the band only, not the facing.

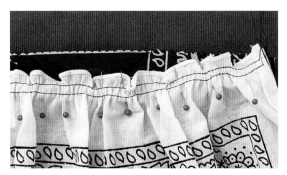

2. With a needle and contrasting-color thread, baste the skirt to the yoke along the gathering lines and remove the pins.

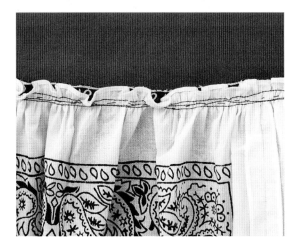

3. Set the machine's stitch gauge to the normal stitch setting. Sew the skirt to the yoke along the basting stitches.

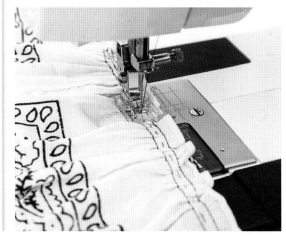

4. Remove the basting stitches with a seam ripper. Press the seam, front and back.

5. On the inside of the tunic, fold under the yoke facing ½″ and pin the folded edge in place along the seamline, tucking the edges in at the center front.

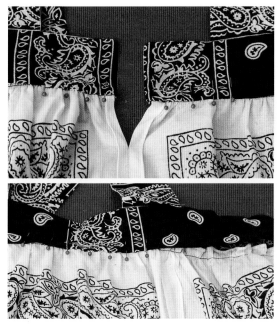

6. With a needle and thread, sew the facing into place using the slipstitch (page 42).

7. At the bottom edge of the skirt, fold a 1½˝ hem to the wrong side of the skirt and stitch the hem into place.

8. To make the ribbon closure, cut the ribbon into 4 pieces each 12˝ long. Fold over 1˝ at the end of each ribbon. Pin 2 ribbons into place on either side of the yoke facing so that they line up. Hand sew the folded ends into place.

9. Trim the ribbon ties to the desired length. Add beads or charms to the ends if you like.

5 Color Your Room:
Pillows

If your room is giving you the blahs, maybe a fresh jolt of color is all that's missing.

With a few bandanas, you can jazz up your bed with a bright choice of pillows.

Shim-Sham Pillow

With its trimmed border, the Shim-Sham Pillow looks a lot like the block-printed fabrics of Provence, France. Not surprisingly, the look of those traditional French fabrics was also influenced by Indian paisleys 200 years ago. Made with two bandanas, this pillow is the same on the front and back.

Things You'll Need

- ☐ Steam iron
- ☐ Sewing scissors
- ☐ Dressmaker's pins
- ☐ Sewing machine
- ☐ Needle and thread
- ☐ 10″ pillow form

MAKE THE SHAM

▶**1**. Press both bandanas and trim off the plain borders.

▶**2**. Line up the bandanas with the right sides together and pin them along 3 sides.

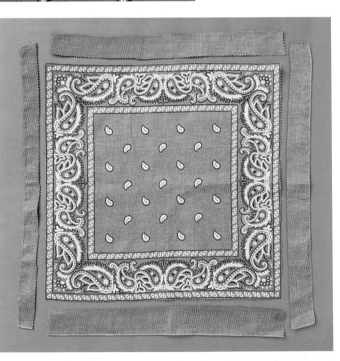

Shim-Sham Pillow

3. Using the border as a guide, machine stitch the bandanas along the 3 pinned sides. See Squared Corners (page 74) for instructions on how to sew corners.

4. Trim the 2 sewn corners to reduce the bulk inside when you turn the sham right side out.

5. Turn the pillow sham right side out and press the seams to make crisp edges and corners.

6. Pin the layers of the sham together along the inner edge of the border of the 3 stitched sides.

7. Sew the sham along the 3 pinned inner borders. You can do this on the machine or by hand. If you sew it by hand, use a running stitch (page 21), but make the stitches and the spaces between them ⅛″ instead of ¼″.

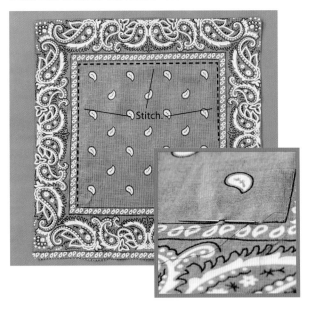

▶**8**. Insert the pillow form.

▶**9**. Pin the layers of the sham together along the open edge of the *inner* border. Fold in the outer raw edges of the sham ¼″ and pin the folds together.

Pin.

Fold and pin.

▶**10**. Sew the inner border with a ⅛″ running stitch. Join the front and back of the sham along the outer edge with an overhand stitch (page 69) or a slipstitch (page 42).

LEVEL:
Medium

BANDANA COUNT:
1

Things You'll Need

- ☐ Steam iron
- ☐ 15″ or 16″ square pillow form
- ☐ Dressmaker's pins
- ☐ Needle with thread in a color to match bandana
- ☐ Scissors
- ☐ Sequins and seed beads *(optional)*

X-Factor Pillow

This pillow is made from a single bandana, and no machine sewing is required. The dark purple color I chose seemed to call for a scattering of silver and gold sequins. With the instructions included here, you can add sequins to any project in this book; after all, they go with everything.

note
If you want to add sequins to your pillow cover, sew the sequins onto the bandana first (see Sewing on a Sequin, page 93). Then continue with the following steps for the pillow.

MAKE THE PILLOW

▶ **1**. Press the bandana and lay it flat, right side down. Center the pillow form diagonally on the bandana, as shown.

2. Fold the corners of the bandana to the center of the pillow. The hemmed edges should just meet, or overlap the tiniest bit. Pin in place.

3. Sew the edges of the bandana, working from the center outward toward each corner. Use the slipstitch (page 42) or overhand stitch (page 69), your choice. Make the stitches neat and small so they're barely visible. That's all there is to it.

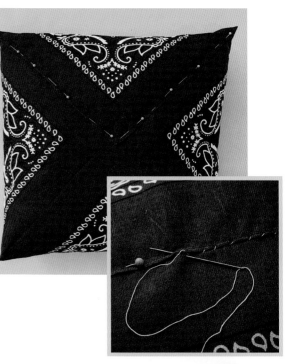

Razzle Dazzle ▷▷▷

There is nothing difficult about sewing on sequins, but I admit, the process is a little slow. If you want your pillow done yesterday, skip the sequins. However, if you have the patience, sequins are worth the effort. Set aside some time when you're listening to music or watching a movie, and add some dazzle to a favorite project. The touch of Bollywood glitter brings the bandana's paisley print back to its origins in India.

Sewing on a Sequin

1. Spread the bandana flat, right side up, and determine where you want to add the sequins.

2. Thread the needle and tie a knot at 1 end. Push the needle from the wrong side of the bandana fabric so it pokes up through the point where you want to start.

3. Place a sequin over the point of the needle and then add a bead.

4. Pull the thread up through the sequin and bead. Turn the needle and head back down, passing along the outside of the bead and through the hole on the sequin only.

In addition to whatever color sequins you choose, you'll need tiny glass seed beads and a needle and thread. Since sequins are made with a single hole, the beads are needed to hold the sequins in place.

Tiny beads have a tiny hole and will require a thin needle with a very small eye. If you have a package of general-purpose needles, choose the smallest one. Put the beads and sequins in small bowls or saucers for easy access and be sure to sit somewhere with good lighting.

5. If the next sequin will be added within an inch of the first, simply point the needle back through the fabric and repeat Steps 3 and 4.

6. The stitches on the back side of the fabric should not be too long—no more than about 1″. Long stitches can easily snag and break, causing the sequins to fall off.

7. When you're done in 1 area, tie a finishing knot (page 22) on the wrong side of the fabric and cut the thread.

TIP

The smaller the needle, the trickier it can be to thread. Be sure to sit in a well-lit space. Trim the thread with sharp scissors. Moisten the tip of the thread and pull it tight between your thumb and index finger to stiffen it. Hold the thread fairly close to the cut end as you poke it through that tiny eye of the needle.

6 Fun and Functional:
Box, Wrap, Book Cover, and Guitar Strap

You'll have fun making these bandana gifts for friends and family, and you can always keep one for yourself!

BANDANA COUNT:

1

will cover 4 small boxes or 2 medium-size boxes.

Things You'll Need

- ☐ Measuring tape
- ☐ Sewing scissors
- ☐ White craft glue
- ☐ Watercolor brush
- ☐ Water for rinsing the brush
- ☐ Lace or grosgrain ribbon trim
- ☐ Small piece of heavy paper
- ☐ Pencil
- ☐ Craft scissors

Dresser Box

Most craft-supply stores stock papier-mâché boxes in various sizes—ready to be decorated any way you like. I chose heart-shaped boxes, but they're also available in round, square, oval, rectangular, and star shapes. The small ones are perfect for storing fortunes from fortune cookies. The larger ones might do for your jewelry or barrettes. No sewing required.

COVER THE BOX

▶**1**. Remove the box lid. Measure the height and circumference of the box. Cut a strip of bandana that is at least 1″ longer and 1″ wider than the measurements.

▶**2**. Drizzle glue over the outer sides of the box and spread it thin with the brush. The surfaces should be thoroughly covered but without any wet pools of glue.

TIP

With glued crafts, be sure to rinse and dry your fingers between steps. You'll save yourself a lot of time cleaning up the finished project. If gluey finger marks do appear, wait until they dry thoroughly, and then wipe them clean with a lightly dampened cloth. (Don't forget to rinse your brush in cool water when you're done!)

Dresser Box

3. Beginning at a corner or at the back of the box, center the strip of bandana and begin wrapping it around the box, smoothing it with your fingers as you go. Allow the strip to extend ½″ beyond the top and bottom edges. You will be surprised at how easily the bandana bonds with the papier-mâché.

4. When you reach the point where you started, go past it a bit and fold the edge of the bandana strip under. Trim off the extra, and glue the folded edge down so it overlaps the first edge.

5. On the inside of the box, brush a ½″-wide coating of glue around the top rim. Fold the top edge of the bandana strip over the rim and smooth it into place with your fingers.

6. Turn the box over. With the point of your scissors aimed toward the box, clip the edge of the bandana strip to make "tabs" at the curves and corners. The tabs will allow you to fold and glue the bandana smoothly over those areas. Glue the bandana around the bottom of the box, smoothing it with your fingers.

7. Cut a piece of bandana slightly larger than the lid of the box. Coat the lid lightly with white glue and place it on the piece of bandana. Smooth any bubbles or wrinkles with your fingers.

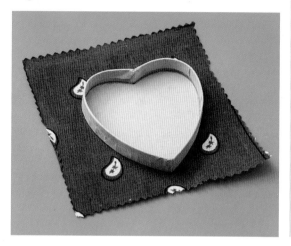

8. Working your way around the lid, coat the outer rim with glue, and fold and smooth the bandana to cover it. Trim the bandana around the edge of the lid, leaving enough fabric to fold inside. Brush a thin coat of glue around the inner rim of the lid. Fold the fabric over the edge and smooth it into place inside.

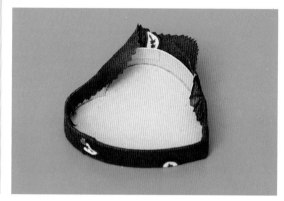

9. For a little extra color, trim the outer rim of the lid with ribbon or lace. Starting at the back of the box, squeeze a thin line of glue around 1 side of the lid. Line up the ribbon along the glue and press it into place with your fingers until it holds. Then squeeze a thin line of glue around the next side and continue until you are back where you started. Trim the ribbon, fold over the end, and glue it in place to hide the starting point. For a finished look, do the same with the inside rim of the box.

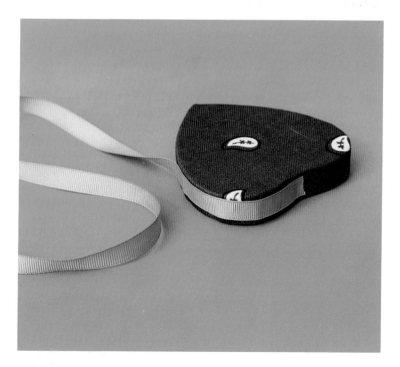

10. Trace the base of the box onto a piece of heavy paper; then cut out the shape with craft scissors. Glue the cutout onto the bottom of the box to cover the bandana edges. Use the surface for writing your gift message.

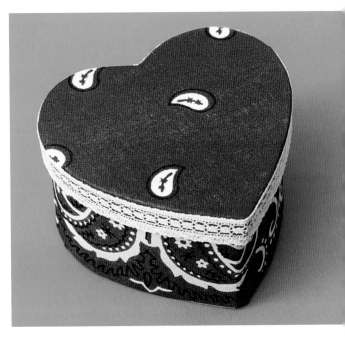

TIP

Want to stretch your gift budget? Plain papier-mâché boxes cost only a dollar or two, and so do bandanas. Put the two together with a little tender loving care, and you'll have a gift that looks like you bought it at a fancy boutique. With so many bandana color choices, you can pick the perfect combination for everyone on your list.

Bandana Gift Wrap

Not only are bandanas handy for making gifts, but they also make the best gift wrap. They're 100% recyclable and suitable for all occasions, and everyone will say how clever you are when you present your gift.

Since gifts come in all shapes and sizes, you'll have to experiment when you wrap yours. But that's part of the fun of bandana wrap. If you don't like the way the package looks the first time you wrap it, simply undo it and try it another way— no ripping, no wrinkling, no problem. Although all packages will be different, a few general tips follow.

Things You'll Need

- ☐ Steam iron
- ☐ Double-sided tape
- ☐ Dressmaker's pins
- ☐ Ribbon
- ☐ Scissors

GET WRAPPING

▷ **1**. Press the bandana and lay it flat on your work surface, wrong side up.

▷ **2**. Center the package on the bandana and see what happens when you fold the sides up and over the top. Although with paper wrap you'd normally overlap the edges on the bottom of the package, with a bandana it's better to have the edges on top so you can make use of the borders.

▷ **3**. Apply double-sided tape to hold the bandana in place. You can pull the bandana away from the tape and reposition the bandana as often as you like.

Bandana-rama—Wrap, Glue, Sew

4. Some packages can be wrapped on the diagonal.

5. Tuck the ends in before folding the sides into place to get rid of extra length.

6. Experiment. Keep tucking and folding until you find a look that you like.

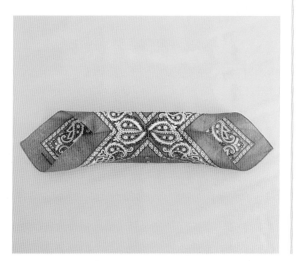

7. Use dressmaker's pins to hold folds in place. Remove them after you've tied the gift with ribbon.

8. Use contrasting ribbon colors to accentuate the designs you've created.

TIP

Bandanas are great for all sorts of gift giving. Coordinate bandana colors for holiday themes. Use a bandana to line a gift basket before you fill it with goodies. Or wrap a vase in a bandana, tying it with ribbon around the neck of the vase; then add flowers, toiletries, art supplies, or whatever suits the giftee!

Book Cover

Your private journal will be even more personal with a custom cover. You'll love the feel of the cotton bandana in your hand, and the wrap-around pocket is perfect for holding photos, magazine clippings, notes, and other bits of inspiration. Best of all, the cover takes only minutes to fold and slide into place.

LEVEL:
Easy

BANDANA COUNT:

1

per book

MAKE THE BOOK COVER

▶**1.** Press the bandana and lay it flat on your work surface, wrong side up.

▶**2.** Make an S fold horizontally across the bandana, so that the book fits comfortably within the borders. Fold the bottom of the bandana up in the middle and then back down, making a 2″–3″ overlap across the middle.

S fold   S fold

▶**3.** Press the fold. This will form the wrap-around pocket.

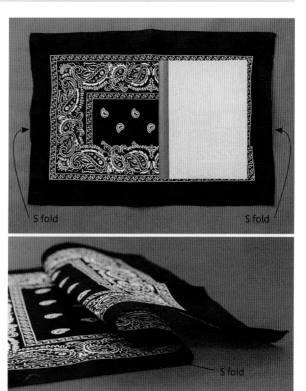

S fold

Side view of S fold

Things You'll Need

☐ Steam iron

☐ Needle and thread

☐ Scissors

Bandana-rama—Wrap, Glue, Sew

4. Lay the bandana wrong side up. Fold over the top and bottom borders of the bandana and press the folds. The space between the top and bottom folds should be just a tiny bit deeper than the book.

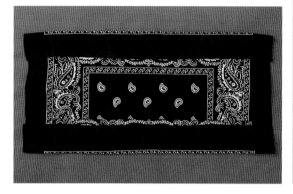

5. Slip the ends of the book cover into the channels created by the top and bottom folds. Adjust the fit until the bandana cover is centered perfectly and fits the book snugly. Crease the new folds along the left and right sides of the book.

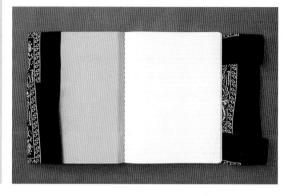

6. Use the needle and thread and a slipstitch (page 42) or an overhand stitch (page 69) to join and reinforce the cover corners, at the top and bottom, front and back.

TIP

Keep the steam iron handy as you make this book cover. Use your fingers to crease the folds to fit the size of your book, then remove the book and press the bandana, using an iron. You'll get the best results if you press the folds at each stage.

Braided Guitar Strap

This braided strap has a great look, and it's padded for comfort on your shoulder. I've rated it "a little tricky" because you might need the help of someone with sewing experience to add the leather strap ends.

Things You'll Need

- ☐ Steam iron
- ☐ Sewing scissors
- ☐ Sewing machine with presser foot and zipper foot
- ☐ 2 rectangular buckles or belt rings, about 2″ wide
- ☐ 2 large paper clamps (also called binder clips)
- ☐ Piece of leather, at least 4″ × 5″
- ☐ Ruler

- ☐ Chalk pencil
- ☐ Dressmaker's pins
- ☐ Needle and thread
- ☐ Wedge-point (leather) sewing machine needle *(optional)*
- ☐ Leather punch *(optional)*
- ☐ 18″ length of flexible cord or narrow ribbon *(optional)*
- ☐ A helpful friend *(optional)*

MAKE THE GUITAR STRAP

▶ **1**. Press the bandanas and cut each in half. You'll only be using 3 halves of each color.

▶ **2**. Select 3 pieces of a single color. On the machine, sew the halves together end to end, leaving a ¼″ seam allowance, to make a strip about 65″ long and 11″ wide. Repeat with the other 2 colors.

Braided Guitar Strap

3. Press the seams open. Fold over the long raw edges about ½″ and press.

4. Set out the buckles or belt rings.

TIP

Buckles and belt rings are available in fabric stores that sell buttons and notions. Any of the types shown here will do. I assembled these and their mates by cannibalizing some old shoulder bags I was ready to get rid of. If you do a lot of sewing and crafting, be sure to remove buttons and hardware from old clothing and accessories before you throw them out—you'll find ways to use them.

5. Lay out the 3 bandana strips, 1 on top of the other. Accordion-fold 1 end of the strips to the width of the buckle opening.

6. Secure the folded end with a paper clamp.

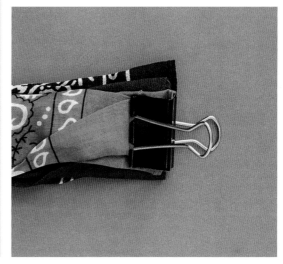

7. If you have a friend handy who can hold the clamped end while you braid, great. Otherwise, place the end in a drawer and shut the drawer so that it holds the strips securely. Step back and begin braiding the 3 colored strips evenly. Hold the strips taut as you continue braiding.

8. When the braiding is complete, clamp the end, remove the braid from the drawer, and set it aside.

▶**1**. Place the piece of leather wrong side up. Measure the width of the buckle opening. Measure, mark, and cut 2 strips of leather, about 4˝ long and the width of the buckle opening.

TIP

Most craft stores sell small pieces of leather that are easily cut with sewing scissors, but the leather elbow patches sold at fabric stores will work just as well for this project.

▶**2**. This is where you'll need the help of an experienced sewist. Replace the presser foot with the zipper foot on the sewing machine. Replace the regular machine needle with a wedge-point needle if necessary. Insert 1 of the leather strips through the buckle about 1˝ and fold it toward itself. Position the strip under the zipper foot on the machine, as shown.

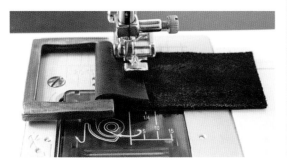

▶**3**. Sew across the end of the leather strip, locking it with forward and backward stitches at either end.

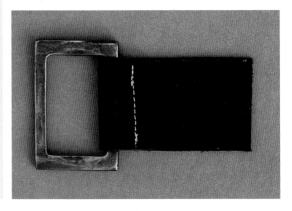

▶**4**. Repeat Steps 2 and 3 with the other leather strip and buckle.

▶**5**. Measure, mark, and cut the free ends of the leather strips into a point, as shown.

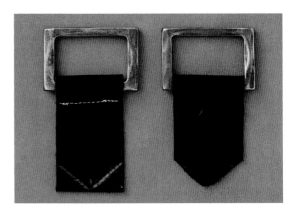

6. Center a leather punch about ½˝ from the point on 1 leather strip; punch a hole. Repeat with the other strip.

7. Make a tiny cut at the top of the punched hole with sharp scissors, as shown. This will allow the hole to open up, so that you can slip it over the strap button on your guitar. Make the cut as short as possible and try it on the button. Then make the cut a little deeper if you need to.

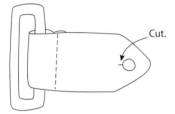

Cut.

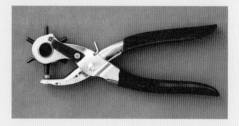

TIP

Leather punches are available at craft and sewing stores. They have adjustable heads for punching holes of different sizes, so they are useful for many projects. But if you don't have one and all of this leather work seems intimidating, you can still make a guitar strap. Simply bring the pieces of leather and the buckles to a shoe-repair shop and have a cobbler stitch and punch the strips for you. Presto! Job done.

PUT IT ALL TOGETHER

1. Remove the clamp from 1 end of the braided bandanas and slip the end through the buckle.

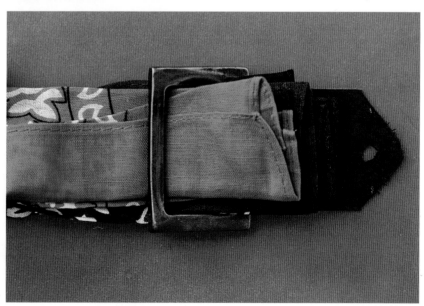

▶ **2.** Fold the end of the braid over and pin it in place. If the fold is too bulky, trim the ends of the bandanas from the middle layer. Sew the fold securely with a needle and thread. Repeat with the opposite end of the strap. You're ready to rock.

 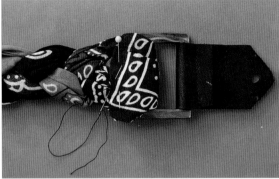

note

Different types of guitars have different setups for attaching straps. Electric guitars usually have two strap buttons, one on the base of the guitar and one at the side of the neck. Acoustic guitars often have just a single button, located at the guitar's base. To attach the strap to the neck of a guitar with no neck button, fold a length of narrow cord or ribbon in half. Thread the folded end through the hole at one end of the guitar strap. Slip the ends of the cord through the fold and pull tight. Tie the cord to the neck of the guitar.

7 Getting Edgy:
Pocket Necklace and Scarf

Hand-stitched edging can be both pretty and practical. Use the stitches to bind the raw edges of fleece or felt, to join two layers of fabric together, or simply to add a decorative trim in matching or contrasting colors.

BANDANA COUNT:
Borders from

2

different-colored bandanas

Things You'll Need

- ☐ Steam iron
- ☐ Sewing scissors
- ☐ Ruler
- ☐ Sewing machine
- ☐ Lightweight fusible woven interfacing
- ☐ Chalk pencil
- ☐ ⅛″-wide ribbon
- ☐ Dressmaker's pins
- ☐ Needle and thread
- ☐ Embroidery thread
- ☐ Small button
- ☐ 30″ jewelry chain
- ☐ Pliers or wire snips
- ☐ Turning tool *(optional)*

Pocket Necklace

This little necklace measures about 3″ × 4″, just the size for tucking away a few small secrets. I purchased the chain at a craft store, but you might also use a chain or beads from an old necklace or even a narrow length of colorful ribbon.

MAKE THE POCKET

▶ **1**. Press the 2 bandana fabrics. Start with the bandana color you want to use for the pocket flap and interior. Starting from the hemmed edge, cut a strip from the paisley border about 3½″ wide and 11½″ long for the pocket interior. Cut a second piece for the flap, about 3½″ wide and 3½″ long. From the second color bandana, beginning at the hemmed edge, cut a strip from the paisley border about 3½″ wide and 9″ long.

▶ **2**. On the machine, sew the flap to the unhemmed end of the 9″ strip, leaving a ½″ seam allowance. Press the seam open. Trim the strip so that it measures 3½″ × 11½″.

Pocket Necklace

3. Cut a piece of fusible interfacing 3½˝ × 11½˝. Iron the interfacing onto the wrong side of the pieced strip from Step 2.

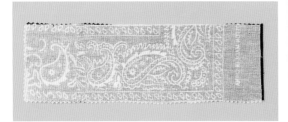

4. Use the ruler and chalk pencil to draw the flap point. Mark the midpoint on the end of the flap (A). Measure 1¼˝ down on either side and make a mark (B). Draw lines from A to B on either side, and then trim the point with scissors, about ¼˝ outside the lines.

MAKE THE BUTTON LOOP

1. Lay the pieced strip right side up. Cut a 3˝ piece of ⅛˝-wide ribbon for the loop. Fold the ribbon in half and pin it to the flap point, with the loop facing inward.

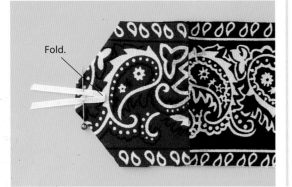

Fold.

2. With the needle and thread, make 1 or 2 stitches near the flap point to hold the ribbon in place. Leave the ends of the ribbon long for now. Remove the pin.

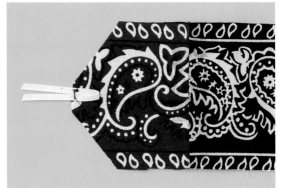

3. Pin the pieced strip to the interior strip with the right sides together and the hemmed edges lined up evenly.

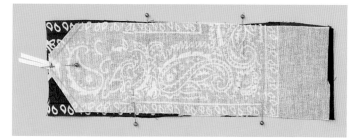

4. On the machine, sew the sides and the pointed end of the strip with a ¼″ seam allowance, leaving the hemmed end open. Trim the seams and the ends of the ribbon.

5. Turn the piece right side out. Insert a turning tool, if helpful, to gently push out the points and edges of the flap.

6. Press the piece. Fold the hemmed edge up to the flap seamline, and press the flap along the seamline.

Blanket Stitch

While most stitching doesn't call attention to itself, the blanket stitch, used for embroidery and edgings, doesn't mind being noticed. In fact, it looks its best when it's stitched in a color that contrasts with the fabric. Make the stitches small, with embroidery floss, or big, with yarn.

1. Thread the needle and insert it through the wrong side of the fabric to hide the knot.

2. For each subsequent stitch, you'll insert the needle through the right side of the fabric, bringing the point out again at the edge. Keep the thread from the previous stitch *under* the point of the needle as you draw the needle through, so that the stitch covers the edge.

3. When you've finished a line of stitching, knot the thread on the wrong side of the fabric.

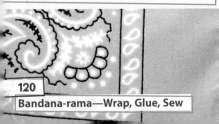

PUT IT ALL TOGETHER

▶**1.** With the needle and a double strand of embroidery floss, work the blanket stitch along the side edges of the pocket, joining the front and back. Hide the starting and finishing knots inside the seam.

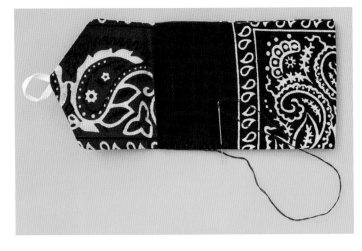

▶**2.** Turn the flap down to determine the location for the button. Sew the button into place (see Sewing on a Button, page 121). Sew through 2 layers only. Do not sew through the back of the pouch.

3. Use the pliers to trim the chain to the desired length to fit over your head, about 25″ to 30″. Sew the ends of the chain to either side of the pocket opening.

Pocket Tee

Follow the steps for the pocket necklace to make a pocket for your favorite shirt. For this shirt pocket, I left out the fusible interfacing to keep the fabric light and flexible. I eliminated the button and button loop and added a charm instead. After pinning the pocket into place, I attached it by sewing the blanket stitch through all the layers, all the way around the pocket.

Sewing on a Button

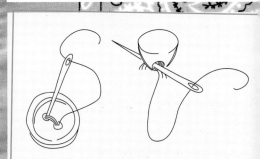

One of the most useful things you'll learn in sewing is how to sew on a button. You'll appreciate that the next time you lose one. Special threads are made for sewing buttons onto coats and jackets, but for this project and for any lightweight clothing, regular poly/cotton thread is fine.

1. Mark the spot where you want the button to go. Thread a needle with a single strand of thread and tie a knot at the end.

2. Bring the needle up from the wrong side of the fabric to the right side, at the marked spot.

3. Thread the needle through the button. For a flat button with holes, you'll pass the needle up through a hole and then back down through the next hole and the fabric. For a shank or pearl button, you'll pass the needle through the hole and back down through the fabric.

4. Repeat several times for a good hold; then finish with a small knot on the wrong side of the fabric.

LEVEL:
Medium

BANDANA COUNT:
3

Things You'll Need

- [ ] Sewing scissors
- [ ] Dressmaker's pins
- [ ] Steam iron
- [ ] ½ yard of 60″-wide fleece
- [ ] Yarn
- [ ] Darning needle

Fleece Scarf

This scarf is as cozy as a winter blanket on one side and as vibrant as a sunny day on the other. I've used fleece for the fuzzy side because it doesn't fray when cut, so there's no need to turn over the edges and add thickness. The pieces go together quickly, but the hand sewing takes a little time. You might want to do it in a couple of sessions. These directions produce a scarf that is about 10½″ wide and 53″ long.

MAKE THE SCARF

▶ **1**. Lay out 3 bandanas, side by side. Trim off the plain borders of the edges where the bandanas abut, to within ½″ of the paisley borders.

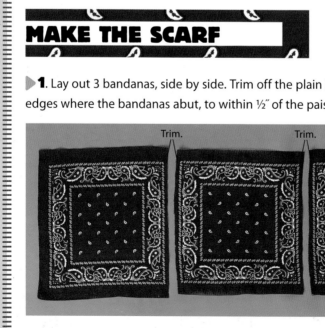
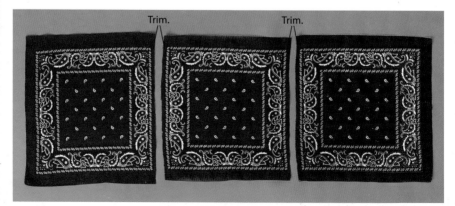

Trim.   Trim.

Fleece Scarf

2. Line up the bandanas along the trimmed edges, with the right sides together. Pin the edges, carefully matching the borders; then stitch along the inner line of the borders.

3. Press the seams open. Lay out the joined bandanas as a long strip and trim off the outer paisley borders.

4. Fold the edges of the bandanas to the wrong side, all the way around. Make the folds about ½" along the long sides and 1" on either end. Press the folds.

5. Spread the fleece material on your work surface, wrong side up. Lay the long strip of bandanas on top of the fleece with the wrong sides together. Pin the 2 fabrics together along each edge, and trim the fleece to match the bandana dimensions.

6. Thread the darning needle with a length of yarn no more than 18″ long. Knot the end and sew a blanket stitch (page 120) around the edge of the scarf. Make the stitches about ½″ deep and spaced about ½″ apart.

TIP

Hide the knotted ends of the yarn between the two layers of fabric. Each time you thread the needle with a fresh piece of yarn, start it under the bandana's ½″ fold, so that the needle point emerges right on the folded edge.

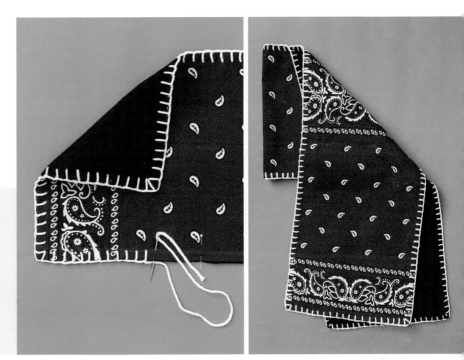

note

Darning needles are the giant version of hand-sewing needles. When you need to sew with yarn, ribbon, or string, the big eye of a darning needle makes it easy.

Winter Blooms

Brighten a gray winter's day by sewing a bandana rose (page 24) or two onto your favorite ski cap. The look is as fresh and unexpected as roses blooming in the snow.

Supplies and Resources

iHome Wholesale • ihomewholesale.com

This website has the absolute best prices for bandanas. It also has an
incredible range of colors. You do not have to be a wholesaler to buy
from iHome; anyone can purchase bandanas on the website, but you
do have to buy a dozen at a time. The website offers packages of "a
dozen mixed light colors" or "a dozen mixed dark colors" as well as
single colors. The delivery is very quick and dependable.

Mood Fabrics • moodfabrics.com

Yes, this is the fabulous store you might have seen on *Project Runway*.
It has just about everything a sewist might need, and the products
are available online too. In addition to fabrics, the store stocks
ribbon, elastic, buttons, pins, pillow forms, machine needles, thread,
professional-grade scissors—you name it, Mood Fabrics has it. The
employees are really nice and helpful too.

M&J Trimmings • mjtrim.com

This is one of my favorite shops in New York. Half of the store is devoted to buttons; the other half is devoted to ribbons, lace, and other trimmings. It sells tapered plastic headbands (three to a package), buckles and D-rings, no-roll elastic, and sequins and beads in every color.

Michaels • michaels.com

If you live near a Michaels, you're already aware that it's a great source for all things crafty. Go to the Michaels website to see if there is a store near you. For this book, I found the heart-shaped papier-mâché boxes there, the chain for the mini pocket necklace, and of course, ribbons and beads.

C&T Publishing • ctpub.com

C&T Publishing, the publisher of the best and most beautiful quilting and sewing books available, also offers a line of useful sewing materials. Its products are available at many fabric and quilt stores, as well as online. I used C&T's Shape-Flex all-purpose woven fusible interfacing for the belt and shoulder bag. I also found Alex Anderson's 4-in-1 Essential Sewing Tool very useful. It includes a seam ripper, a turning tool, a fold presser, and a stiletto for piecing quilts.

About the Author

Judith grew up in a sewing family and has been lucky enough to combine her love for art and needlework with her career as a writer. She has written for publications on Cape Cod and in New York and developed award-winning children's craft and activity books for the Metropolitan Museum of Art.

Photo by Alexis Procopion

Her earlier books have included _What Can You Do with a Paper Bag?_, _Can You Find It?_, _Museum ABC_, _Beads: A Book and Kit_, and _Write Like an Ancient Egyptian_. This is her first book with C&T Publishing. She lives and works in New York City.